Girl with Cat,
1989, Fernando Botero (to find out more see page 41)

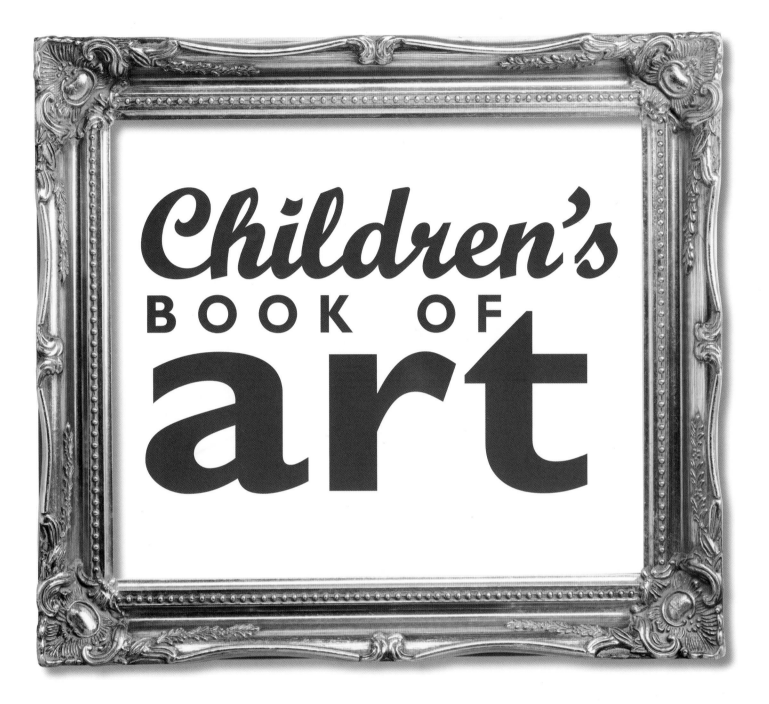

Children's
BOOK OF
art

LONDON, NEW YORK,
MELBOURNE, MUNICH, and DELHI

Senior designers Sonia Whillock-Moore
and Pamela Shiels
Senior editor Deborah Lock
Additional editing by Anneka Wahlhaus
Sue Malyan, Lorrie Mack, Elizabeth
Haldane, Wendy Horobin, Penny Smith
Additional design by Mary Sandberg,
Gemma Fletcher, Rachael Grady,
Clemence De Molliens, Sadie Thomas
Art director Rachael Foster
Publishing manager Bridget Giles
Production editor Sean Daly
Production controller Claire Pearson
Jacket designer Jess Bentall
Jacket editor Mariza O'Keeffe
Picture researchers Jo Walton
and Julia Harris-Voss

Art consultants Rebecca Lyons,
Art Historian and Lecturer for Christie's
Education and National Gallery, London
and Emily Schreiner, Manager of Family
and Children's Programs at the
Philadelphia Museum of Art, USA

First published in the United States in 2009 by
DK Publishing
375 Hudson Street, New York, New York 10014

Copyright © 2009 Dorling Kindersley Limited,

09 10 11 12 13   10 9 8 7 6 5 4 3 2
CD276 – 07/09

A catalog record for this book
is available from the Library of Congress.

ISBN 978-0-7566-5511-2

Color reproduction by Media Development
Printing Ltd., UK
Printed and bound by Leo, China

Discover more at
www.dk.com

Jacket images: *Front:* **The Bridgeman Art Library:**
Monasterio de El Escorial, Spain / Giraudon tr (Durer);
Musee Conde, Chantilly, France / Giraudon tl (Book of
hours); Private Collection/Christie's Images c (Degas);
Van Gogh Museum, Amsterdam, The Netherlands /
Giraudon br (Van Gogh); **Corbis:** Burstein Collection bl
(Hokusai); Marco Simoni / Robert Harding World Imagery
(Gaudi); ©The Andy Warhol Foundation for the Visual
Arts t (Warhol); **Lasar Segall, 1891 Vilna - 1957 São
Paulo, Collection of the Lasar Segall Museum, São
Paulo, National Institute of the Historical Artistic
Patrimony, Brazilian Ministry of Culture:** c (Segall)

How to use this book

In this book, find out about different art
styles, the works and lives of famous artists
and sculptors, the way some artworks
were created, and the amazing range of art
around the world. There are four different
types of page in this book:

*ARTIST or SCULPTOR PROFILE: Find out about
the life, style, and work of a famous artist or
sculptor and take an up-close look at a work.*

*HOW DID THEY DO THAT? Find out how an
artist or sculptor did their work and see how
the technique developed through history.*

*GALLERY: Marvel at the different ways artists
around the world and throughout art history
have portrayed the same subject.*

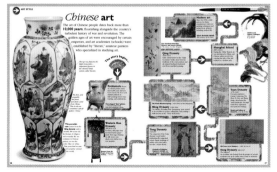

*ART STYLE: Find out about the different styles
of art and follow the timeline of changing
styles through art history.*

Contents

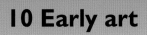

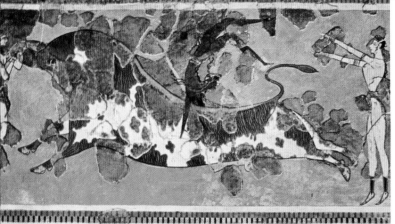

What is *art*?

This is a **tricky question** to answer, because art can be so many things:

It's not just drawing

... but can also be **collage**, mosaics, **prints**, **PHOTOGRAPHY**, *sculpture*, video, painting, and many other media.

It's not just h☺ppy...

but can also show **anger**, *pain*, wonder, **SADNESS**, and many other emotions.

It's not just acceptable...

but can also be **rebellious**, controversial, *dramatic*, and spiritual.

It's not just pretty...

but can also be horrifying, scandalous, and challenging.

"Painting is poetry that is seen rather than felt..."
(Leonardo da Vinci, Renaissance artist, see page 34)

It's not just in **galleries**

... but can also be in **churches**, public buildings, in parks and on the streets, in magazines—**in fact, there's art all around you**.

It's not just an **image**...

but can also be a **meaningful idea** and a **historical source**, informing us about the lifestyle of people in the past and present.

It's not just REALISTIC

... but can also be abstract, symbolic, imaginary, distorted, or a fleeting impression of a moment in time.

It's not just for art **lovers**...

but also for **all** people of **all** ages to react to.

10

From the first images on cave walls to dramatic masterpieces hanging in exhibitions, the **story of art** takes us around the world and traces the developments in artistic skills, materials, and style.

Rocky beginnings

In the beginning, there was cave art—the markings of **prehistoric man.** Although thousands and thousands of years old, the drawings are beautifully preserved, often found deep inside a mountain or underground, safe from being worn away by the weather. Imagine in the dim glow of a flickering fire, cavemen using **burned sticks** or **dirt** mixed with a little water to create their beautiful paintings.

> I'm a bull from the Lascaux caves in France. I'm 17 ft (5 m) long!

European cave art
The impressive cave art found at the Lascaux caves in France is also known as the **"prehistoric Sistine Chapel"** (see page 19). The caves were discovered in 1940 by four teenagers, who were said to be chasing their dog, Robot.

> No one knows what the paintings were for. Maybe as decoration or graffiti, or for ceremonies or passing on information? What do you think?

The wall's texture shapes the animals.

> We were painted 15,000 years ago.

African cave art

The walls of the desert caves in Libya, Africa, are covered with pictures of giraffes and other grazing animals. These paintings suggest that in **12,000 BCE**, when they were created, the now-barren Sahara Desert was a lush, tree-filled landscape.

The only animals that live in the Sahara Desert today are camels, snakes, and small mammals.

The vast sand dunes of the Sahara Desert as they are today.

Drawing of a prehistoric African hunter and his dog

Black markings were made using charcoal. This is wood that has been buried under sand and then burned.

American rock art

This art is found at Newspaper Rock in Utah. It was created by American Indians before 150 CE. Rather than painting the rock and the marks gradually washing away over time, the people scratched the oily surface to reveal the lighter sandstone underneath for a lasting image. These images are called **petroglyphs**.

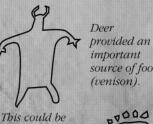

Deer provided an important source of food (venison).

This could be a spirit figure, or possibly a witch doctor.

Feet and tracks show a journey.

13

Papyrus paper

Ancient Egyptians were the first to make paper, using papyrus, a plant once found along the banks of the River Nile. Papyrus was also used to make ropes and baskets.

To make paper, the green skin of the papyrus stalks was removed and the stalks cut into long strips. The strips were flattened out and then some were laid horizontally on a cotton sheet.

Other strips were placed vertically on top. This gave the crisscross pattern found in papyrus paper. Then the strips were pressed. The natural juice of the papyrus plant acted as a glue to seal all the strips together, creating a single sheet of paper.

Egyptian scribes

For the ancient Egyptians, art had a specific purpose rather than just decoration. In general, most art was designed to ease the journey through the **afterlife** or to worship the gods. Egyptian scribes had a very strict set of rules to follow when painting. Erwin Panofsky, a German art historian, discovered that Egyptian scribes used a **mathematical system of grids** to make sure all figures were drawn in proportion.

The eyes and shoulders of Egyptian figures were shown facing the front, but all other parts of the body were shown side on.

Nebamun's tomb painting

Nebamun was an official in ancient Egypt. Around his tomb was a large wall painting. This scene showed Nebamun with his family **hunting birds** in the marshes of the River Nile. This type of scene, showing the deceased doing something they enjoyed, was very common in tombs. Nebamun wanted this wall painting in his tomb so that he could have lots of birds and fish to hunt in the afterlife, a place for the dead to live.

Can you see the cat balancing on two reeds trying to catch birds? Cats were family pets in ancient Egyptian times but also used as hunting partners.

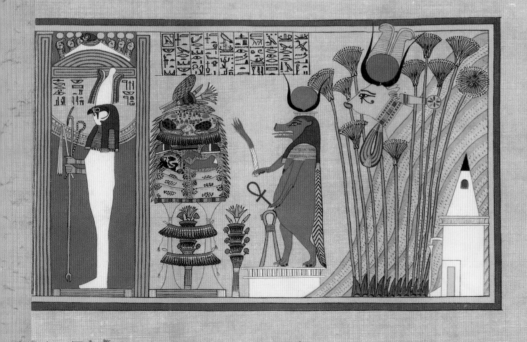

Book of the Dead

The ancient Egyptians were often buried with their own **Book of the Dead** to ensure they passed safely through the Underworld, to be reborn into a new life. The book would contain a range of texts, including spells, and small illustrations known as **vignettes**. The vignettes were very important as they showed what would happen in the afterlife.

▲ **Summer,** 1573, Giuseppe Arcimboldo, **Oil on canvas** Arcimboldo became famous for his clever portraits of human heads, using fruit, flowers, and vegetables for every season.

▲ **Portrait of an Infant,** **20th century, Tsuguji Foujita, Oil on canvas** Foujita, from Japan, is well-known for mixing Eastern and Western painting styles to create his own style. He was influenced by artistic movements in Paris and eventually changed nationality to French in 1955.

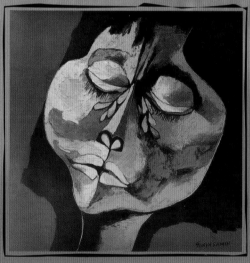

▲ **Niña Llorando,** 20th century, **Oswaldo Guayasamín, Oil on canvas** The Ecuadorian artist, Guayasamín, painted over 100 pictures showing the subject of pain and suffering of the local people living in the Andes.

▲ **Self portrait with black background,** **1915, Helene Schjerfbeck, Oil on canvas** Throughout her life, the Finnish painter Helene Schjerfbeck painted her own face. This one shows her at 53 years old, but later she painted herself as a frail old woman, nearing death.

◄ **Hip mask** c. 1600, Benin, Nigeria, **Ivory** This mask would have been worn by an African king at a special ceremony held to remember his mother. The face is carved from ivory and looks like the image of a real woman.

How to make frescoes

Crushed rock for paint colors

Fresco is one of the methods used for painting a picture onto a wall or ceiling. **Pigments**, the materials that make the color, are painted onto a surface covered in plaster. Frescoes have been found on the walls of ancient Egyptian tombs and used to create amazing effects on the ceilings of cathedrals.

Roman style

The Romans used a technique called **buon fresco** (true fresco) to decorate the walls of their buildings. Powdered pigments such as natural brown and red earths were mixed with water and painted onto the surface of wet plaster, made from lime and sand. As the surface dried and hardened, the pigment **blended in** to color the plaster. The artist had to work very quickly before the plaster dried.

Portrait of Terentius Neo and his wife, *1st century—Fresco from Pompeii, Italy*

In the dry climate of Italy, some Roman frescoes have survived. The ones at Pompeii were preserved when the volcano Vesuvius erupted and buried the city in 79 CE.

The owner of the house, Terentius Neo, was a baker who wanted himself and his wife shown as successful and clever. He holds a scroll to show he can read.

The wife holds a stylus (a writing tool) and an open diptych (an ancient writing tablet) and looks as if she is about to finish off some writing.

ASK YOURSELF
... If you were in a painting, what objects would you hold? What might they say about you or your hobbies?

A writing tablet (diptych)

Fresco timeline

The fresco technique was used by ancient people all over the world. The technique has, over time, become popular again.

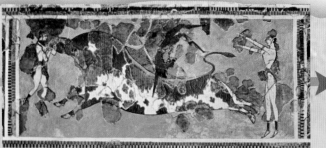

17th century BCE *This bull-leaping fresco was on the walls of the ancient Great Palace at Knossos on the island of Crete.*

1st century *This fresco of a baker and his wife who lived in Pompeii, Italy, was preserved by volcanic ash.*

14th century *The walls of the Arena Chapel in Padua, Italy, are covered in frescoes by Giotto di Bondone and his assistants. The figures, which are about half the size of a person, look three-dimensional.*

The strong red colors were made from sienna, a hard red rock found in the Italian hillsides.

Here's how to make a Roman fresco

After preparing the wall with a layer of rough plaster, the Roman fresco artists would create the painting bit by bit as the pigment needed to be applied onto wet plaster.

Roman fresco from inside a villa in Pompeii

1 *Crushed pigments made from rocks and dried plants were mixed with lime water to form the paste.*

2 *A small patch of fine wet plaster called the intonaco was put on to the wall.*

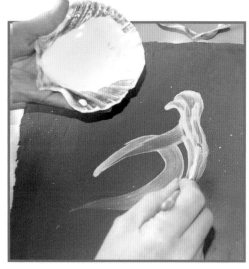

3 *The paste was painted on right away. Since the plaster was still wet, the pigment would bond with the plaster.*

4 *Once the picture was completed, wax was put over the surface to protect the picture and make it shine.*

1541 *It took Michelangelo four years to complete the famous fresco on the ceiling of the Sistine Chapel in the Vatican in Rome, Italy.*

1688–1694 *The huge fresco ceiling in St. Ignazio Church, Rome, by Pozzo is an impressive illusion.*

1896 *This is one of six large frescoes at the National Museum in Stockholm, Sweden, painted by Carl Larsson.*

1933 *The Mexican painter Diego Rivera used fresco for his* Detroit Industry *series (detail).*

Dreamtime art

For thousands of years, Aboriginal people have been creating art, including body and bark painting, clay and wood sculptures, and rock art. Some surviving rock engravings are about 40,000 years old.

Dreamtime

According to traditional Australian aboriginal belief, the world was created during a magical period known as the "dreamtime." To aboriginals, the dreamtime is not in the past but is a parallel stream of time running through past, present, and future. In the dreamtime, ancestral beings rose from beneath the Earth and wandered across the landscape, creating the mountains, valleys, and rivers we see today.

X-ray paintings
At Ubirr, northern Australia, there are rock paintings that show skeletons, lungs, and other internal organs. Many of these pictures are of animals eaten by Aboriginal people—turtles, kangaroos, and fish—and are part of a hunting and fishing magic.

This rock painting, in Northern Territory, Australia, shows a **creation-ancestor**: a humanlike spirit with large eyes and no mouth. Many rock paintings are repaired and repainted during religious rituals.

Aborigines make paints from natural plants and minerals such as this red and yellow ocher. They grind it to powder, mix it with liquid, then paint using bark or sticks.

To paint an X-ray picture, an artist often began by drawing a white silhouette, then filled in the details with ocher paints and charcoal.

Technique

Ancient Aboriginal painters used **earth colors**—reds, browns and yellows, black and white—made from natural plants and minerals. A variety of ways were used to apply the paint. Some pictures were painted using fingers, the palm of the hand, sticks, or feathers. Grasses, chewed twigs, narrow strips of stringy bark, or palm leaves were also used to make brushes. For **stencil designs**, the paint was blown out of the mouth around an object.

An Aborigine bark painting of a hunter and a kangaroo.

Charles Inkamala works on a painting in Alice Springs, Australia.

The principal motifs of contemporary dreamtime art are circles, semicircles, spirals, dots, and lines. Ancestors are portrayed in simple lines and geometric designs.

Contemporary art

Today, artists continue to explore their culture, land, and dreamtime. Many use modern materials, including watercolors and acrylic. However, they combine these with traditional earth colors. They also use traditional **dot painting** techniques, and curved and wavy lines.

Modern artist, Clifford Possum Tjapaltjarri (1932–2002), used dots and circles to create large, complex works of art.

A goanna painted to honor its ancestral spirit.

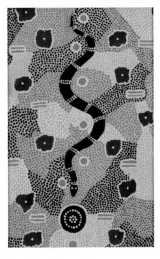

Snake Dreaming *was painted in 1989 by artist Keith Kaapa Tjangala.*

An assortment of gold and silver glass tesserae

Tesserae made of natural stone and marble.

How to make mosaics

Mosaic is the art of creating images with small pieces of colored glass, stone, pottery, or other hard material. These small tiles or fragments are called **tesserae**. From the first pebble designs, to the glittering effects of the Byzantine art, to the textured modern abstracts, mosaics have covered the insides and outsides of buildings with **stunning effect**.

Byzantine style

Glass tesserae in many different colors, including **gold** and **silver**, were used on the walls and ceilings during the Byzantine period (330–1453). This art was mainly based on religious Christian themes and, by **tilting** the tesserae, light would reflect from the haloes and faces of the holy people.

How to make a mosaic

Byzantine mosaicists would have placed the tesserae directly into a bed of lime cement, working a section at a time because the cement would dry quickly.

Try making a mosaic yourself. Draw your design onto a wooden base. The Byzantines had to work quickly, but give yourself more time by applying the tile adhesive piece by piece.

2 *Use special tile cutters to shape each piece of tessera so they fit together well and follow the curves of your design. Tilt each one a little so it will catch the light.*

3 *Byzantine mosaics were never grouted (filling the spaces between the tiles with fine cement), but a fine layer applied to your design will seal it and make it stronger.*

Mosaic timeline

The ancient Greeks in the 4th century BCE began the craze of making mosaics, using different-colored pebbles to create patterns and scenes. Here are some of the designs since then.

1st century *Marble and limestone tesserae were used in Roman floor mosaics.*

6th century *The large floor mosaic in the Great Palace of Constantinople (now Istanbul) used 80 million tesserae.*

7th century *Islamic mosaics have repeating patterns of rich blues and greens as on The Dome of the Rock in Jerusalem.*

12th century *The nave of the Norman cathedral of Monreale in Sicily is covered from end to end with Byzantine-style mosaics of glass tesserae.*

Hagia Sophia, Istanbul (detail from the face of Christ),
6th century—Glass tesserae

The Hagia Sophia in Istanbul, Turkey, is an excellent example of Byzantine art and architecture, but only a few of the mosaics have survived, such as this one of an emperor kneeling before Christ.

Beneath the huge dome of the Hagia Sophia were mosaics of prophets, saints, and other religious figures. This face of Christ was made up of specially manufactured tesserae called **smalti**, which were cut into cubes from large, thick sheets of colored glass. No grouting was used between the pieces, so as to allow light to reflect the color within the glass.

Adding some sparkle

For silver or gold leaf smalti, thin sheets of silver or gold were put between two slabs of glass to make a **mirrorlike** piece. This was then cut into smaller pieces and placed at a slight angle to the wall. These pieces then sparkled, as they reflected the light in different ways.

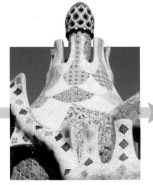

1900–1914 *Antoni Gaudí's vibrant, multicolored mosaics cover Park Güell in Barcelona.*

1957 *The Mexican muralist Diego Rivera designed the huge glass mosaic on the outside wall of the Teatro de los Insurgentes in Mexico City. The image shows a visual history of theater and dance in Mexico.*

1977 *The mosaics of Jeanne Reynal have different-sized tesserae, making a rough texture.*

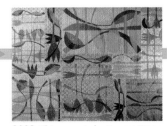

2008 *This mosaic by Emma Biggs was stuck to a kitchen wall with cement-based adhesive.*

Gods and heroes in art

Artists and sculptors have been inspired by **ancient legends** and **religious stories**. These pieces show the brave deeds of mythical heroes and the great works and lives of religious figures.

SEEING THINGS
For more on stone carvings see page 106

▶ **St. George and the Dragon,**
c. 1470, Paolo Uccello, Tempera on panel This painting shows the legend of St. George defeating the dragon and rescuing the princess.

▲ **In The Dream World,**
1995, Norval Morrisseau, Acrylic on canvas According to an American Indian tribe called the Ojibwe, the color blue protects the human spirit from danger.

▶ **Hercules and Nessus, 1599, Giambologna, Marble**
Giambologna was a highly skilled sculptor famous for carving dramatic scenes. Here, Hercules, the ancient Greek hero, is about to beat his opponent the centaur, Nessus.

◀ **The Hero Overpowering a Lion, c. 725 BCE, Assyrian, Stone**
This carving is thought to be the mythical hero Gilgamesh demonstrating his superhuman powers by controlling a ferocious lion.

Le Héros Gilgamesh
Palais de SARGON à KHORSABAD (VIIIᵉ siècle)

▲ Taglung Thangpa Chenpo

c. 1300s, Tibet, Ground mineral pigment on cotton
Tibetan monks would carry painted or embroidered banners like this one during ceremonial processions. Buddhas, teachers (lamas), and other gods surround Chenpo, the founder of the Taglung monastery.

▲ Orpheus playing to the animals, Roman

artist, Mosaic Ancient Greek legend says that Orpheus, a mythical poet, was so talented a musician that he was able to tame wild animals.

SEEING THINGS
For more on Renaissance art see page 30

◄ The Baptism of Christ, 1450s, Piero della Francesca, Tempera on panel

The dove, seen above Christ, represents the Holy Spirit. Paintings such as this were painted to decorate altars, churches, and chapels.

◄ First Avatar of Vishnu as "The Fish"

19th century, Indian, Painted and gilded wood Vishnu, the Hindu protector god, is shown rescuing the world from a flood and so saving all the people.

Chinese art

The art of Chinese people dates back more than **10,000 years**, flourishing alongside the country's turbulent history of war and revolution. The golden ages of art were encouraged by certain emperors, and art academies (schools) were established by "literati," amateur painters who specialized in studying art.

The top row features the Eight Immortals—important figures in the Chinese belief system called Taosim.

The first, and arguably the finest, porcelain came from China. This is why we sometimes call all pottery "china."

This porcelain vase comes from the **Qing dynasty** and is around 300 years old. Its themes of religion and everyday life are common in Chinese pottery, as was the color: blue on white. This porcelain became very popular around the world.

The story begins...

Prehistoric Pieces of colored pottery more than 6,000 years old have been found with faces and animals painted on. Cliff paintings show wars, hunting, and celebrations.

Three-legged "Kuei" pitcher, *c. 3rd–2nd century BCE, from the Longshang Culture*

Western Han Dynasty
206 BCE–9 CE
In China, silk paper was invented before paper made from rags. Painting on silk woven into sheets and clothes was very popular.

Banner from the Tomb of Dai Hou Fu-Ren, *c. 180 BCE*

Modern art
Since the 1950s, artists such as Liu Haisu experimented with new painting techniques and painted new subjects, including modern life.

Yellow Mountain (detail), *20th century, by Liu Haisu*

Chicken and Chinese Cabbages, *20th century, by Qi Baishi*

One Hundred Butterflies, Flowers, and Insects (detail), *17th century, by Chen Hongshou*

Qing Dynasty
1644–1911
Some artists known as the "Eight Eccentrics" broke away from the traditions of the court painters and developed freehand brushwork and flower-and-bird painting.

Shanghai School
20th century
During the 1900s, Western art was introduced to China, and Chinese artists moved from copying the style of the old masters to a modern style.

Yuan Dynasty
1279–1368
Four great painters— Huang Gongwang, Wu Zhen, Ni Zan, and Wang Meng—developed the "mind landscape" through which they expressed their personal feelings.

Woods and Valleys of Mount Yu, *1372, by Ni Zan*

The Peach Blossom Spring, *c. mid-1500s, by Wen Zhengming*

Ming Dynasty *1368–1644*
The literati, including Wen Zhengming, were trained to be excellent at poetry, calligraphy, and painting— skills known as the "Three Perfections."

Tang Dynasty
618–907
The emperors of the Tang dynasty (royal family) enthusiatically supported artists. Figure paintings of nobles and court ladies became a major theme.

Portraits of Thirteen Emperors (detail), *late 7th century, by Yan Liben*

Old Trees, Level Distance, *c. 1080, by Guo Xi*

Song Dynasty *960–1127*
The Imperial Art Academy was formed from the merger of several academies set up in earlier times. Their art included landscapes that looked almost 3-D.

How to create colors

Très Riches Heures du Duc de Berry (detail from April), 15th century, by the Limbourg brothers—Vellum

Today you can buy tubes or jars of paint in just about every color you can imagine. But over six hundred years ago artists had to **mix up** their own colors. They would buy the paint in the form of a colored powder, or **pigment**, and then mix it with a liquid binder. These are some of the pigments that may have been used to create the **illuminated manuscript** shown here:

Tempera paint

Artists' workshops in the **Middle Ages** were busy places. The apprentices would prepare the materials and colors, while the main artists painted. This is how tempera paint—mainly used on **wooden panels**—was made:

1 *The dry pigments were ground and mixed with water to form a paste. This was skilled work, since grinding some pigments too much could spoil the color.*

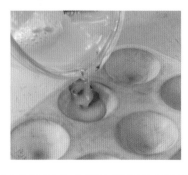

2 *Egg yolk was separated from the white, pierced and collected in a container. A little water was added before the egg yolk was mixed with the pigment paste.*

Orange

The mineral cinnabar was crushed to make the orange-red color. This contained mercury, which is now known to be slowly poisonous.

Blue

The deep rich blue color called ultramarine was more expensive than gold because the rock lapis lazuli was imported from Afghanistan. It was reserved for painting the regal gowns and the amount to be used was specified by the patron of the work in the contract.

Gold

Gold was the most expensive color after ultramarine. It was beaten into very thin sheets to make gold leaf.

Gold leaf was applied to the picture and then made shiny by "burnishing" it with a stone.

Black

By burning animal bones in a sealed container, a pigment of deep blue-black to brown-black color was produced. This was called bone black.

Green

When copper is exposed to air over time a brilliant green coating forms called verdigris. This coating was used by artists in their paintings. To make verdigris, artists left a real copper coin in a dish of vinegar.

The copper was melted, cooled, and then separated into shavings to be ground into powder for pigment.

White

The brilliant opaque white of the white garments was painted in lead white. It was a very common pigment manufactured from metal. The lead content made it poisonous if a person was in contact with it for long. It has now been replaced by zinc or titanium.

Pink

The purple-red color came from a plant dye made from the root of a plant called madder. The madder roots were dried in the sun and then ground into a powder.

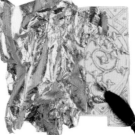

Sunflower head with seeds

Purple

Crushed sunflower seeds made the lilac shade of the color purple.

Dried pieces of Madder root

Renaissance (1400s–1500s)

The story of **Western art** covers the art of Europe (and later the Americas). In the **15th century**, the classical skills and ideas of the ancient Greeks and Romans were rediscovered and inspired a new art style called the Renaissance, meaning "rebirth."

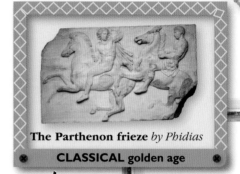

The Parthenon frieze by Phidias
CLASSICAL golden age

In the 1st century, the influence of Roman art and culture spread across Europe and northern Africa. Statues, frescoes, and panels were detailed and lifelike.

Around 500 BCE–300 BCE, the art of the ancient Greeks flourished. Artists produced marble sculptures (see page 114), black- and red-figure vase painting, and painting on wooden panels (few of which survive today).

A fresco from Pompeii, Italy, *1st century*

A mosaic from the Hagia Sophia, Istanbul, *6th century*

Saint George, *c. 1415–17, by Donatello*

MEDIEVAL art

470–1453 The now-established Christian religion became a main subject of art across Europe. In the east, **Byzantine art** continued the traditions of the classical art styles.

Around 1410, the artists in the Netherlands began to use linseed oil (made from flax seeds) and walnut oil mixed with pigments, making **oil paint**.

Classics REBORN

In the early 1400s, there was renewed interest in all things classical. The Italian artists Donatello, Alberti, Brunelleschi, and Masaccio created the **Renaissance style**. Donatello's sculptures show the lifelike and detailed poses and expressions of the Roman sculptures.

In western Europe, wealthy aristocrats known as patrons were prepared to pay for art that showed off their wealth. Painters set up **workshops** and hired assistants to help them with illuminated manuscripts and wooden panels.

Trés Riches Heures, *15th century, by the Limbourg brothers*

Around 1413, the architect Filippo Brunelleschi developed the **rules of perspective**. This was adopted by artists such as Masaccio in their work to create the illusion that their paintings had depth.

After studying Roman architecture, Filippo Brunelleschi designed and built the impressive dome of Florence Cathedral, Italy (right), between 1419 and 1436.

The Tribute Money, *c. 1425, by Masaccio, shows linear perspective, where the eye is drawn to a single vanishing point because many lines appear to meet there. The most important part of the painting, the figure of Jesus, has been positioned here.*

Rules of PERSPECTIVE

Artists around Europe developed their Renaissance styles...

Italian

Sandro Botticelli
Portrait of Guiliano de' Medici, *1478–80*
One of Botticelli's patrons was the Medici family, who were wealthy merchants and rulers in Florence.

Raphael
The School of Athens (detail of the Greek philosophers Plato and Aristotle), *c. 1509-10*
In addition to Leonardo da Vinci and Michelangelo, Raphael was one of the most famous artists of the High Renaissance, a period where artists were considered to have achieved artistic perfection.

Titian
Assumption of the Virgin, *1518*
In Venice, Titian proved he was an impressive painter with this huge and complex altarpiece.

Northern European

Jean Fouquet
The Melun Diptych (detail), *c. 1452*
The French painter Fouquet painted figures with sharp, severe features.

Rogier van der Weyden
The Braque Triptych (detail), *c. 1452*
Using attention to detail, van der Weyden gave his figures realistic expressions. Other Netherlandish painters such as Jan van Eyck (see page 36) did the same.

Pieter Brueghel the Elder
Fight between Carnival and Lent (detail), *1559*
The Netherlandish artist Brueghel painted lively crowded scenes, adding witty details and using lots of color.

German

Albrecht Dürer
Self portrait, *1498*
Dürer combined both the detailed style of northern Europeans with the color, light, composition, and perspective of the Italian style.

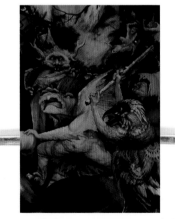

Matthias Grünewald
The Isenheim Altarpiece (detail), *c. 1512–15*
With his fearsome demons, Grünewald was influenced by medieval art. He used bright, expressive colors.

Hans Holbein the Younger
The Ambassadors, *1533*
Holbein was well-known for his large magnificent portraits. Here he showed the people surrounded by objects that displayed their wealth and power.

▲ **Bociany (detail),** 1900, Józef Chełmonski, **Oil on canvas** Bociany is the Polish word for storks, which are very common in Poland.

◀ **Hunters in the Snow (Winter),** 1565, **Pieter Brueghel the Elder, Oil on panel** This is one of a series of six paintings called "The Seasons," which shows a landscape changed by different seasons.

Landscapes in art

Although **landscapes** were often subjects of Chinese art, it was not until the Renaissance that Western artists such as Brueghel (above) began to develop this subject, which has since become very popular.

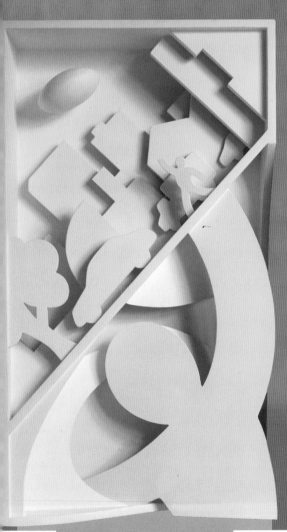

▲ **Summer Evening on the Skagen Southern Beach with Anna Ancher and Marie Krøyer,** 1893, **Peder Severin Krøyer, Oil on canvas** This piece by the Norwegian painter Krøyer shows a peaceful and serene summer evening walk along a beach in Denmark. His wife and a friend are in the painting.

◀ **Tilted Landscape,** c. 2003, **Michael Buhler, MDF, plywood and acrylic** In his constructions, Buhler combines everyday activities with a paranormal experience, such as this tilting urban scene.

▲ **Winter Landscape,** c. 1470s, **Toyo Sesshu, Ink on paper** Sesshu developed his own style of Japanese ink painting by making landscapes with bold strokes.

▲ The Trees, c. 1906, André Derain, Oil on canvas
Derain helped create Fauvism, which is a French art style using lots of bright colors. The colors in this painting are used to create a sense of the bright sunlight on the landscape.

◄ Early Spring, 1917, Tom Thomson,
Oil on wood panel Thomson was one of the artists who started up the "Group of Seven." This group of artists celebrated Canada's natural beauty in their paintings.

▲ The Cornfield,
1826, John Constable, Oil on canvas England's great landscape painter often painted scenes of Suffolk, remembering the area where he grew up.

▲ Surge of Spring, 20th century, Emily Carr,
Oil on canvas Often working outdoors, Carr passionately painted the landscape of British Columbia, Canada. Her expressive paintings showed the power of nature.

▲ The Sun, 1912–16, Edvard Munch, Oil on
canvas This painting is part of a mural at the Oslo University, Norway. The light of the sun in this painting is dazzling, which grabs the attention of the viewer.

SEEING THINGS
For more on Edvard Munch see page 69

33

Artist's biography
Leonardo **da Vinci**

1452: *Born near Vinci in Tuscany, Italy*

1472: *At age 20 joined the fraternity of St. Luke in Florence as a painter*

1473: *Painted the* Annunciation, *possibly his earliest surviving painting*

1481: *Painted the* Adoration of the Magi

1483–1499: *At age 31 moved to Milan and worked at Duke Ludovico Sforza's court*

1495–1498: *Painted the* Last Supper

1499: *Left Milan to travel and returned to Florence in 1500*

1502–1503: *Worked for Cesare Borgia as a military engineer*

1503–1506: *At age 50 painted the* Mona Lisa

1516 or 1517: *Left Italy for France, as invited by the king, Francois I*

1519: *Died in Cloux in France*

Artist's influences

Andrea del Verrocchio —*Studied in Verrocchio's studio as an apprentice, and was inspired by* **the classical past,** *and a fascination with* **anatomy**, **landscape,** *and* **light**

Portrait of Lisa Gherardini, wife of Francesco del Giocondo, *1503–1506, 30 x 21 in (77 x 53 cm)—Oil on poplar wood*

Leonardo **da Vinci**

"I have offended God and mankind because my work did not reach the quality it should have."

Leonardo was a great artist, as well as a scientist, an engineer, a thinker, and a musician. His wide range of talents made him the original **Renaissance** man. He designed war instruments and his notebooks contain technical and anatomical drawings and **scientific studies**. This side of his work was undiscovered for centuries, and Leonardo is predominately known for his painting and drawing.

Inventions

Leonardo was fascinated with how machines worked. He studied all of the machines of his time and then designed and developed new ones. His ideas were **ahead of his time**, such as a helicopter, a machine gun, and even a tank.

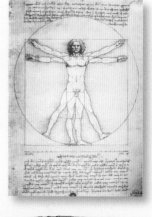

This study of human proportions from Vitruvius's De Architectura *was sketched by Leonardo.*

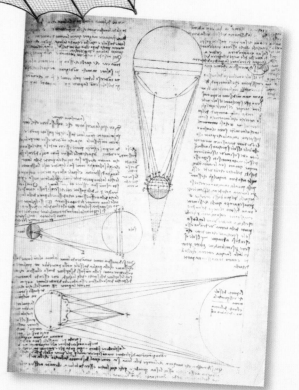

This is a model based on Leonardo's sketch of an ornithopter, a flying machine with mechanical wings.

Captivating mystery

Usually known as the *Mona Lisa*, this portrait (which is believed, but not known, to be of Lisa Gherardini) has enchanted generations of adults and children. Along with her **mysterious smile,** one of the most intriguing elements of the painting is the strange and **haunting scene** behind her, with its bridge and winding road leading to a wild and uninhabited landscape beyond.

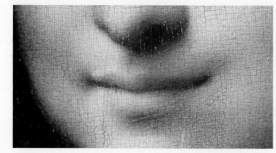

Leonardo developed the technique of *sfumato*, a subtle way of dealing with light and shade through the **blurring** of tones and colors (*sfumato* means smoky). He blended the edges of the Mona Lisa's lips into her skin in a natural and lifelike way.

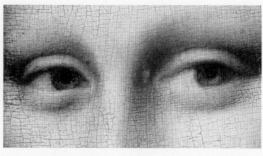

Also defined with *sfumato*, the model's eyes seem to have no brows or lashes. The lady's gaze seems to follow the viewer no matter where he or she stands to look at the painting.

These are Leonardo's notes and sketches about the size of the Earth and the Moon and their distances from the Sun. The words around the sketches were written in mirror-writing.

Artist's biography
Jan **van Eyck**

We know almost nothing of van Eyck's early life. His career as an artist is documented only from 1432, when he would have been 42 years old.

c. 1395: *Born around this time, possibly in Maaseik, near Maastricht, Netherlands*

1422: *Worked in The Hague at the court of the Count of Holland*

1425: *Settled in Bruges as painter to Philip the Good, Duke of Burgundy*

1426: *Death of van Eyck's brother Hubert, an equally respected painter, who had been working on Jan's renowned* Ghent Altarpiece

1428-1429: *Traveled to Portugal on a diplomatic mission for the Duke of Burgundy*

1432: *Completed the* Ghent Altarpiece

1433: *Produced his* Portrait of a Man, *thought to be a self-portrait*

1441: *Died in Bruges, Belgium*

Artist's influences

Illuminated manuscripts
—*Inspired by precise style and attention to detail*

Portrait of a Man, *1433, Oil on wood*

Jan **van Eyck**

Jan van Eyck is the most **respected artist** of the early Netherlandish school. His reputation, established within a few years of his death, has never dimmed. Once (wrongly) credited as the "inventor" of oil painting, he did develop a brilliant technique for **glazing** that allowed him to create rich colors and the impression of depth and texture. The work of Jan van Eyck had a **profound influence** on generations of painters of many different styles and nationalities.

Portrait of prosperity

While *The Arnolfini Portrait* (full title **Portrait of Giovanni Arnolfini and His Wife**) was once thought to record a wedding, experts now think it is simply the portrait of a **wealthy Italian merchant** and his wife based in Bruges—it may even commemorate her death. Despite appearances, Arnolfini's wife is not pregnant— the shape of her dress and the way she's holding it were very **fashionable** at the time.

The artist left an ornate signature above the mirror in a witty, modern-sounding, style: it translates as "Jan van Eyck was here 1434."

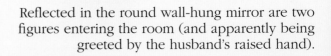

Tiny painted scenes from the life of Christ circle the mirror.

Reflected in the round wall-hung mirror are two figures entering the room (and apparently being greeted by the husband's raised hand).

Some people believe all the objects in this picture have a special meaning. Others think they are just things. What do you think?

The candle above the husband is lit—the one above his wife is not. This may mean that she's dead.

Oranges were very costly in Europe. Together with the fine clothes and luxury furnishings, they may indicate wealth.

The little dog is thought to represent constancy—"Fido," the popular pet's name, is Latin for "I am faithful."

Experts once believed that the kicked-off clogs (used for outdoor wear) meant this room was holy ground.

The Arnolfini Portrait, *1434, 32 x 24 in (82 x 60 cm)—Oil on oak*

How to use oil paint

Fatty oils, made from certain plants such as linseed, poppy, and walnut, harden when exposed to air. These are **mixed** with pigments to make oil paints. In the early 15th century, Jan van Eyck (see page 36) showed how oil paints could create **rich colors**, light, and shade, and, as the paint dried slowly, details could be perfected. Oil painting continues to be popular with artists.

Rembrandt's style

The Dutch artist Rembrandt van Rijn used a technique called **impasto**—thickly applied oil paint— to create depth, richness, and texture in his paintings.

Here's how to paint like Rembrandt

To recreate the colors that Rembrandt used, choose yellow ocher, red ocher, burnt sienna, burnt umber, white, and black paint.

1 *Paint a textured base on a tightly stretched primed canvas. To do this, brush some reddish-brown paint from side-to-side and up and down.*

2 *Using a large hog-bristle brush loaded with thick oil paint, paint on layer after layer. Areas that are to stand out get more layers and lighter-colored paint.*

3 *In certain areas where the paint is very thick, loosely move the paint around with a brush.*

Oil paint timeline

Since the creation of oil paints in the early 1400s, artists have experimented with clever effects in their oil paintings.

1661–62 *Rembrandt built up layers of thick oil paint to create expressive light and shade effects.*

1856 *Sir J. E. Millais was a member of the pre-Raphaelite group who chose to paint in a deliberately detailed style. Later his style loosened.*

1871 *In this portrait of his mother, James McNeill Whistler uses only shades of gray and black, painting "art for art's sake," with no narrative meaning.*

1901 *The Danish painter Vilhelm Hammershøi used white and tones of gray and black to create light and shadow effects in his interiors.*

Self portrait (detail), *c. 1665,*
45 x 37 in (114 x 94 cm)—Oil on canvas

Rembrandt was in his 50s when he painted this picture of himself wearing a turban on his head.

Special effects

In addition to impasto, Rembrandt used an effect called **chiaroscuro**. Areas of strong light, such as faces, are contrasted with areas of heavy shadow, such as clothes. This gave the paintings **depth** and made certain details stand out to the viewer.

On the turban, Rembrandt made broad, thick strokes of white paint.

1928 *One of the leading modern Brazilian artists, Tarsila do Amaral used bright oil colors and tropical images in her paintings, such as* Abaporu.

1937–45 *Roberto Matta, a Chilean artist, used oil paints to create his "automatic" surrealist landscapes (see page 79), allowing his unconscious mind to take over.*

1968 *The Greek artist Yannis Tsarouchis aimed to combine naturalistic color with realistic shading and accurate perspective, such as in* The Four Seasons.

Children in art

These paintings show children doing what they like best; **playing** their favorite games, cuddling their toys, dressing up for a celebration, having lots of fun with friends, and stroking animals!

▲ **Luca, Minerva, and Europa Anguissola Playing Chess,** 1555, **Sofonisba Anguissola, Oil on canvas** Many of Anguissola's paintings were of her family. In this piece, her sisters are playing chess. The detailed embroidery of their clothes shows their family was rich.

▲ **Portrait of a mother with her eight children,** 1565, **Jakob Seisenegger, Oil on panel** Seisenegger, from Austria, was a court painter to Emperor Ferdinand I. He became well known for painting full-length portraits.

SEEING THINGS
For more on Renaissance art see page 30

▲ **Children's Games (detail),** 1560, **Pieter Brueghel the Elder, Oil on wood** This is only part of a much larger painting, which shows lots of children playing. Some children appear to be playing nicely, while others look like they are being spiteful.

◄ **Las Meninas (detail),** 1656, **Diego Velázquez, Oil on canvas** This painting shows the daughter of the Spanish king and queen with her maids of honor (las meninas). She was only four or five years old at the time.

▶ **Mother with Twins,** 1982, **Henry Spencer Moore, Bronze** Moore often created large pieces of abstract sculpture showing a mother with her child, although this is the only one with twins.

▲ **Girl with Cat,** 1989, Fernando Botero, **Oil on canvas** The most noticeable thing about Botero's paintings are the exaggerated size proportions, which are intended to be light-hearted and comical.

▲ **A Day of Celebration,** 1895, Carl Larsson, **Watercolor on paper** Larsson is famous for his watercolor paintings of children playing. He had eight children—they were his favorite subjects for his paintings.

▲ **Child with Birds,** 1950, Karel Appel, **Oil on canvas** Appel was hugely influenced by children's drawings. His works are Expressionist pieces, using bright colors and painted as if by a child.

▶ **Ballet Dancer,** 1921, Edgar Degas, **Dressed (bronze)** Modern-life subjects were the main focus of Degas' art. To make this sculpture look even more lifelike, he used real fabrics for the tutu, bodice, and slippers as well as real hair tied with ribbon. He used wax for the original statue, which was cast in bronze after his death.

▲ **Boy with Lizards,** 1924, Lasar Segall, **Oil on canvas** When Segall moved to Brazil from Germany, he was amazed at the new sights he saw. The boy in this painting is playing with a couple of lizards in the wild.

Baroque (1600s)

Baroque was the name given to the style of art and architecture in the 17th century. **Grandeur, drama, and emotion** were features of the style. Subjects included not just religious art, but also portraits, landscape, myths, scenes of everyday life, and still life.

The story continues...

School of Athens (detail), *1510–11, by Raphael*

Early 1500s
The artists of the **Renaissance** had been inspired by the Classical golden age in ancient Greece and Rome.

After 1520, a new art style called Mannerism developed. It distorted the High Renaissance style with **intense emotion**. Mannerist artists included Jacopo Carucci, known as Pontormo.

MANNERISM

Madonna and Child with Angels and Saints, *c. 1517–18, by Jacopo Carucci (Pontormo)*

Pope Pius IV, *1586–1600, by Bartolomeo Passarotti*

Mid-1500s
In northern Europe, countries broke away from the Catholic Church, setting up Protestant churches and banning religious paintings. In a **Counter Reformation**, the Catholic Church encouraged religious art in southern Europe to promote their Church.

Camera obscura

Picture viewed up-side down for the artist to trace.

Around 1550, an early type of camera was developed known as the **camera obscura**. This device was sometimes used by artists such as Jan Vermeer (see page 44) to help plan their paintings.

Allegory of Music, *c. 1595*

Early 1600s
Caravaggio and Annibale Carracci were two of the earliest **Baroque** painters, working in Rome.

CARAVAGGIO (c. 1571–1610)

In the 1600s, young nobles were expected to tour around Europe for their Classical education. **Rome** in Italy became the hub of all artistic and touristic activity.

The GRAND Tour

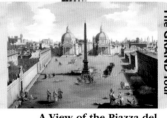

A View of the Piazza del Popolo in Rome, *c. 1700s, by Gaspar van Wittel*

1643-1715
In the reign of Louis XIV of France who was known as "The Sun King," France was the leading power in Europe. He and his French nobles lived together in a lavish **Palace at Versailles**, living in luxury and grandeur.

Baroque artists painted one or more of these subjects...

Religion

Giovanni Francesco Barbieri
The Betrayal of Christ (detail), *c. 1621*
Barbieri was more commonly known by his nickname Guercino ("Squinter"), because he always squinted. He used strong colors, interesting lighting effects, and off-center compositions to create dramatic paintings.

Bartolomé Murillo
Immaculate Conception of the Venerable Ones, *c. 1678*
The Spanish artist Murillo mainly produced religious paintings, using soft colors and giving his figures sweet expressions.

Pietro da Cortona
David killing Goliath,
17th century
An architect as well as a painter, Cortona worked in Italy. His art showed dramatic movements typical of the Baroque style.

Naturalism

Pieter de Hooch
Nursemaid with baby in an interior and a young girl preparing the cradle,
17th century
Typical of Dutch artists of this century, Hooch chose indoor and outdoor scenes from daily life to paint.

Sir Anthony van Dyck
Lady Anne Cecil, *c. 1630s*
Born in the Netherlands, van Dyck traveled around Europe painting portraits of wealthy nobles. He made them look elegant and proud.

Diego Velázquez
The Lunch, *1620*
In all his work, Velázquez made his figures and objects realistic and lifelike. He became the official painter for the king of Spain, Philip IV, and was hired to paint many portraits.

Classicism

Nicolas Poussin
An Italianate wooded landscape,
17th century
Poussin was inspired by the art of the ancient Greeks and Romans. His finest paintings are his landscapes, where the trees and hillsides are idealized and ordered.

Sir Peter Paul Rubens
Achilles Defeating Hector, *1630–32*
Rubens worked for various monarchs in northern Europe. He produced many paintings in every type of subject known at that time.

Claude Gellée Lorrain
Seaport with the Embarkation of the Queen of Sheba, *1648*
The French landscape artist Claude painted Italian landscapes in soft, rosy colors. He charged high prices for his paintings as souvenirs for the travelers on the Grand Tour.

Artist's biography
Jan **Vermeer**

1632: *Born in Delft, Netherlands*

1653: *At age 21 became a member of the Delft painters' guild*

1662: *Elected to be the headman of the painters' guild*

1665-1666: *Painted Girl with a Pearl Earring*

1672: *French invasion of Netherlands caused economic slump that affected the art market*

1675: *At age 43, died in debt and unacknowledged*

1866: *Reputation restored by French art critic Théophile Thoré*

Artist's influences

Pieter de Hooch
—*Contemporary artist who also painted scenes of everyday life and light-filled interiors*

Emanuel de Witte
—*Inspired by calm, light effects in the paintings of church interiors*

The Kitchen Maid, *c. 1658*
Vermeer is famous for "genre" paintings, which feature cozy domesticity and natural light.

Jan **Vermeer**

"He created a world more perfect than any he had witnessed." Art historian Walter Liedtke

Now among the most loved of all artists, Jan Vermeer was **little known** outside of his hometown of Delft during his lifetime, and he didn't achieve universal **recognition** until the late 1800s. As far as we know, Vermeer may not even have been a full-time artist. Certainly, he would have worked hard to support his wife and 11 surviving children, and only about **35 pictures** by him are known to survive.

Picture story

The Art of Painting is a symbolic work (allegory) about painting in the old Netherlands. The model is **Clio**, the muse of history, and the artist (in 15th-century dress) might be Vermeer himself. Like all his work, this picture is remarkable for its **quality of light**. He used tiny dots of paint to suggest the fall of light or the texture of an object. One critic described the surface of his pictures as "like crushed pearls melted together."

To highlight the importance of the painter's art form, Clio's victory wreath "crowns" his hand.

*Clio's trumpet represents the **fame** an artist can achieve. In the book she holds, she makes a record of heroic deeds—Vermeer may be saying that skill as an artist is just as heroic as triumph in battle.*

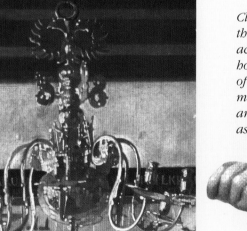

Interior life

Vermeer's rooms are just as important and interesting as his people. The **elaborate** brass chandelier shimmers with his famous dots of light, the floor tiles direct our gaze at the main action, and the hanging carpet adds a **theatrical** flourish. (Can you spot a life-sized mask in the picture?)

The Art of Painting, *c. 1666, 48 x 39 in (120 x 100 cm)—Oil on canvas*

Still life in art

Still-life paintings show **objects** such as fruit, furniture, and flowers. In the 17th century, artists aimed to make the objects look realistic but since then they have used still life to **explore styles**.

◀ **Sunflowers**, 1888, Vincent van Gogh, **Oil on canvas** Yellow is an important color within this painting, since it signified happiness for van Gogh. He painted several versions of the *Sunflowers*, some of which were hung up in the Yellow House, which he rented in Arles, France.

SEEING THINGS
For more on Vincent van Gogh see page 64

▲ **Vanitas**, 17th century, Simon Renard de Saint-André, **Oil on canvas** A vanitas is a type of still-life painting that was popular in the Netherlands during the 17th century. Vanitas paintings often include symbols of the shortness of life; for example, in this piece a skull is used to show death.

▲ **Still Life with Bowls of Fruit and Wine-Jar**, 1st century BCE, Roman, **Fresco** This is part of a larger fresco of fruit and a wine jar found in the house of Julia Felix in the ancient Roman town of Pompeii.

▲ **Still life with Basket**, 1888-90, Paul Cézanne, **Oil on canvas** This is a still-life painting of a basket overflowing with bright fruits. Cézanne completed hundreds of still lifes during his painting career.

Old Models, ▶

1892, William Michael Harnett, Oil on canvas In this painting, Harnett wanted to make the objects as realistic as possible. He has cleverly painted them to look three-dimensional.

◀ Still Life with Porcelain Lamp, 1918, Gabriele Münter, Oil on canvas Münter, a German Expressionist painter, was interested in art from a young age. She became cofounder and the only female member of the art group known as "The Blue Rider."

SEEING THINGS
For more on Cubism see page 69

▲ The Round Table, 1929, Georges Braque, Oil, sand and charcoal on canvas Braque made lots of still-life paintings set on a round table. In this piece, the table is covered in his favorite things. The objects have been fragmented, a style called Cubism. Braque also used sand in this painting to create a weird texture.

▲ Chianti Bottle and Fish, c. 1960s, Fikret Muallâ, Gouache on paper Gouache—paint mixed with a type of gum—was Muallâ's favorite way of painting. It allowed him to work quickly on his still-life paintings.

ROCOCO (1700s)

One of the **main styles of the 18th century** across Europe was called Rococo. This was an **ornamental style** with elegance and fun. The name probably came from the French word *rocaille,* meaning a decorative form of rock-art where shells and pebbles were used to cover fountains.

During the 1700s...

Piazza of St. Peter's in Rome, Italy, designed by the Baroque architect Gianlorenzo Bernini

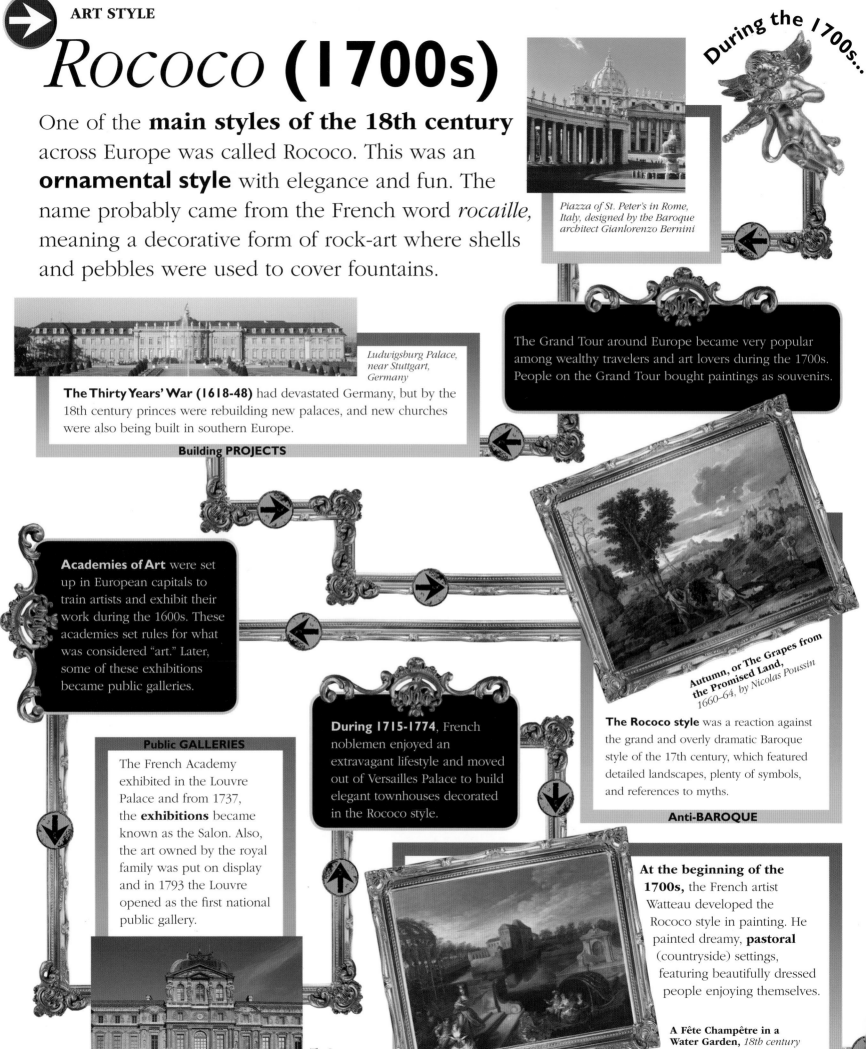

Ludwigsburg Palace, near Stuttgart, Germany

The Thirty Years' War (1618-48) had devastated Germany, but by the 18th century princes were rebuilding new palaces, and new churches were also being built in southern Europe.

Building PROJECTS

The Grand Tour around Europe became very popular among wealthy travelers and art lovers during the 1700s. People on the Grand Tour bought paintings as souvenirs.

Academies of Art were set up in European capitals to train artists and exhibit their work during the 1600s. These academies set rules for what was considered "art." Later, some of these exhibitions became public galleries.

Public GALLERIES

The French Academy exhibited in the Louvre Palace and from 1737, the **exhibitions** became known as the Salon. Also, the art owned by the royal family was put on display and in 1793 the Louvre opened as the first national public gallery.

During 1715-1774, French noblemen enjoyed an extravagant lifestyle and moved out of Versailles Palace to build elegant townhouses decorated in the Rococo style.

Autumn, or The Grapes from the Promised Land, 1660–64, by Nicolas Poussin

The Rococo style was a reaction against the grand and overly dramatic Baroque style of the 17th century, which featured detailed landscapes, plenty of symbols, and references to myths.

Anti-BAROQUE

At the beginning of the 1700s, the French artist Watteau developed the Rococo style in painting. He painted dreamy, **pastoral** (countryside) settings, featuring beautifully dressed people enjoying themselves.

A Fête Champêtre in a Water Garden, *18th century*

Jean-Antoine WATTEAU (1684-1721)

The Louvre Palace

Across Europe, artists painted in the Rococo style...

French school

Jean-Honoré Fragonard
The Swing, *1767*
Fragonard captured the Rococo spirit in his colorful, joyful, and playful paintings, featuring aristocrats having fun.

François Boucher
The Chinese Marriage or An Audience with the Emperor of China, *c. 1742*
Boucher was very popular among the noblemen and royalty of the French court as his paintings reflected their desires in his imaginary settings.

Italian School

Canaletto
Return of the Bucintoro on Ascension Day, *18th century*
Canaletto became famous as a view-painter capturing the grand scenes of festivities on the canals in Venice, Italy. He sold his work to the wealthy travelers on the Grand Tour.

Giambattista Tiepolo
The Education of the Virgin, *1732*
An incredibly quick painter, Tiepolo was known for his frescoes that could create amazing illusions.

Central European School

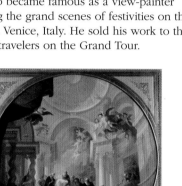

Franz Anton Maulbertsch
Presentation in the Temple, *18th century*
An Austrian artist, Maulbertsch was commissioned to decorate churches and buildings across Europe.

Johann Baptist Zimmermann
The Last Judgment (detail), *1746–54*
One of Zimmermann's greatest works was to decorate the ceiling of Wies Church in Germany.

British School

William Hogarth
Marriage A-la-Mode: IV, The Toilette, *c. 1743*
Hogarth painted sequences of witty paintings, telling stories with moral themes. There were six scenes for Marriage A-la-Mode.

Thomas Gainsborough
Mr. and Mrs. Andrews, *c. 1750*
Many wealthy British people posed for their portraits by Gainsborough. He sometimes set these portraits in a landscape setting.

Artist's biography
Francisco **de Goya**

1746: *Born in Fuendetodos, near Saragossa, Spain. He was the son of a gilder and his art training began with a local painter*

1763: *At age 17 moved to Madrid and then studied in Italy around 1768 to 1771*

1785: *Appointed deputy director of painting at the Royal Academy in Madrid*

1786: *Appointed the King's Painter and became the main painter to the royal household in 1789*

1808–13: *Continued as royal painter under Joseph Bonaparte, who was occupying Spain*

1814: *After the restoration of the Spanish king, painted* The Second of May, 1808 *and* The Third of May, 1808

1824: *Settled in Bordeaux, France, and died there in 1828*

Artist's influences

Goya described himself as a pupil of **Rembrandt** *(self-portrait above), Diego Velázquez, and nature.*

Francisco de Goya

"United with reason, imagination is the mother of all art and the source of its beauty."

Goya was a very versatile painter, best known in his lifetime for **portraits**, (see his self-portrait, *c.* 1797-1800 above). He could show a wide range of **emotions** in his work, he used paint in a very physical way (sometimes thinning it, or possibly applying it with a sponge and spoons), and he was a master of softly shaded layers. An early **Romantic**, he was also fascinated by people, religion, and morality.

This etching was number 43 from the series **Los Capriches**, *a set of 80 etchings published in 1799 about the social and political situation at that time.*

The Sleep of Reason Produces Monsters, *1796–98, Print from etching*

As the central figure throws his arms up in surrender, you can see terror in his eyes.

Romantic spirit
Displaying some of the first traces of Romanticism in his work, Goya often painted the world of **dreams**, and even featured mysterious, dreamlike creatures.

Third of May, 1808, *1814, 104 x 135 in (265 x 345 cm)—Oil on canvas*

A huge lantern provides light for the brutal nighttime slaughter.

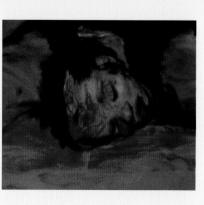

Dying for freedom

During the early 19th century, Napolean's army occupied Spain, Goya's country, but on May 2, 1808, the citizens of Madrid rose up in **rebellion**. The next day, French soldiers shot hundreds of the rebels and many innocent bystanders. Goya was only able to record the **horror** after the Spanish king was restored to his throne several years later.

Goya wanted to show how gruesome and bloody these executions were.

51

How to use
watercolor

Watercolor paint is made from a colored pigment mixed with water. It is applied in **thin washes** of delicate color that are gradually built up. The main quality of watercolors is their transparency and **illusion** of light.

Dawn after the Wreck, *c. 1841, Watercolor, graphite, red chalk on paper*

J. M. W. Turner's style

Joseph Turner was one of the masters of **Romantic** watercolor painting. He became known as the "painter of light" because of his **fascination** for the effects of weather on the sea and sky.

Watercolor timeline

Watercolor probably began with early cave paintings where pigments were mixed with water. They became more popular in the Renaissance and are now widely used by amateur artists.

Here's how to paint like Turner

Turner used the "**wet-in-wet**" technique to cover large areas of the paper with background colors that blend gently into each other.

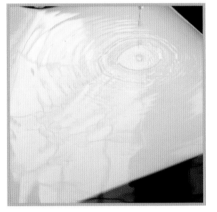

1 Soak the paper thoroughly with water.

2 *The color is applied in loose strokes and allowed to spread.*

3 *Once on the page, the pigment can be diluted with more water, or other colors added. The colors run into each other smoothly.*

4 *Dried breadcrumbs can be used to lift out small spots of color. A clean sponge or rag can be used for larger areas.*

15th century *Albrecht Dürer was one of the first artists to paint landscapes in watercolor. This painting is of Innsbruck Castle, Austria.*

19th century *Turner visited Venice three times. He would make hundreds of sketches and rough watercolors while he was there and paint full-sized pictures when he got back.*

19th century *Dante Gabriel Rossetti's picture* Arthur's Tomb *imitates the style of early Italian artists. The figures are drawn awkwardly and the perspective is wrong, like a medieval illustration.*

There are a number of **techniques** used in watercolor. In addition to wet-in-wet, washes can be left to dry and further colors laid on top to create a depth of color. Areas of the paper are also left white or **scratched** out afterward rather than using white paint.

Turner painted his watercolors in stages. He would cover the paper with large areas of thin color to form the **background**. He would then apply washes of color to define buildings and shapes. Finally, he would use **fine brushstrokes** of thicker paint to add details.

THINK ABOUT...
the types of effects you can get with watercolors. Try mixing colors using the wet-in-wet method and see what happens.

A Canal Near the Arsenale, Venice, *19th century—Watercolor on paper*

20th century *In his picture* Bedouins, *John Singer Sargent draws attention to the finely detailed faces by painting the clothes in loose brushstrokes.*

20th century *Mildred Butler's watercolors often depicted the gardens and landscapes around her home in Ireland.*

20th century *The Chinese artist Qi Baishi used large brushes to capture the spirit of his subject in swift, vigorous strokes.*

20th century *Raoul Dufy's* Horses and Jockeys under the Trees *is typical of the way he would lay down color washes and then add simple outlines to suggest fine detail afterward.*

In the corner is a stamp of some calligraphy characters. This is how Japanese artists signed their work. Hokusai used more than 20 different names during his career, depending on his style at the time.

The Great Wave off Kanagawa, *1829–33*
10 x 15 in (25.9 x 37.2 cm)—Color woodcut

Making a woodblock print

Did you know that the earliest woodblock prints are nearly 2,000 years old? They date back to ancient China in 220 CE. Amazingly the process of making a woodblock print is the same today as it was then!

The image is drawn and placed facedown onto a block of wood.

The areas where the image will be white are chiseled away.

The areas to be printed a particular color are left raised.

Katsushika Hokusai

A traditional print of geishas, c. 1780

In the 1800s, **Katsushika Hokusai** revolutionized Japanese art. He used a woodblock printing technique, but instead of showing samurai, geishas, and nobility—the subjects chosen by other Japanese artists—Hokusai drew **landscapes** and ordinary life in the countryside. He strived for realism, perspective, and movement, which can be seen in his famous print **The Great Wave off Kanagawa.** Copies of this print have been sold all over the world, influencing thousands of artists and designers.

These fishermen, taking fresh fish from their village to the fish markets of Edo (now Tokyo), are caught up in some **powerful ocean waves.** The largest wave with its grasping claws is threatening to engulf the three boats. How do you think the fishermen feel? Are they afraid? Or are they **confident** they'll make it as they have done so many times before?

Hokusai worked obsessively on creating woodblock prints. He created more than 30,000 works, but even at the end of his life he felt he could do better. He signed one of his last works as "The Art-Crazy Old-Man."

Mount Fuji

The Great Wave was one of a series of prints called the *Thirty-Six Views of Mount Fuji* (1829–1833). Although Mount Fuji is in the background of this picture, it is **framed** by the large waves and in the foreground a **small peaked wave** copies its shape.

Artist's biography
Katsushika **Hokusai**

1760: *Born in Edo (now Tokyo), Japan*

1775: *Became an apprentice woodblock engraver*

1778: *At age 18, joined the studio of Katsukawa Shunshõ*

1797: *Adopted the name Hokusai Tomisa and produced brush paintings and illustrated books*

1814: *Created a collection of sketches known as the series* Hokusai Manga

1824-1830: *Produced many famous works, including landscapes*

1849: *Died and buried in Tokyo's Seikyõji Temple at age 89*

Artist's influences

Chinese art —*For 1,500 years, Chinese paintings had featured long-distance landscape views*

Dutch landscape engravings —*Influenced by the use of perspective, shading, and realistic shadows*

The raised image is covered in printing ink and then pressed onto paper.

Different blocks are made for each color and used again to make lots of copies.

Mount Fuji volcano is the highest peak in Japan and according to myths was the source of the secret of immortality and a home to gods.

Modern *art*

1850 onward

In the modern era, artists focused less on the subject matter of their artwork and more on the **artistic process** and sharing their ideas and emotions through their art.

Impressionism

Art was to change forever in 1860s France, when a group of artists invented "Impressionism." Their new approach was to capture the **"impression"** of what is seen at any particular moment. How the picture was painted became just as important as the subject matter. Unable to exhibit their work at the art academies, these artists organized their own exhibitions.

How did it happen?

By the 1840s, ready-mixed paint could be bought in resealable aluminum tubes. This meant painters could complete a painting **outside** more easily, allowing them to capture the light and weather effects on a scene.

Galloping Horse, *1887, by Eadweard Muybridge*

By 1850, photography, invented just over a decade earlier, had developed and become a craze. Later, **motion photography** captured how animals and humans moved. These developments made artists rethink the composition and accuracy of a painting.

Poachers in the snow, *1867, by Gustave Courbet*

In the early 1860s, Edouard Manet used a new way of painting, purposely making his brushstrokes visible on the painting. This approach makes him one of the founders of modern art.

— **VISIBLE Brushstrokes** —

Mother Anthony's Tavern, *1886, by Pierre-Auguste Renoir*

By the late 1860s, a group of French Impressionists regularly met in cafés in Paris to discuss their ideas and techniques. Often the cafés themselves became subject-matter.

In the 1850s, Gustave Courbet, and other painters, began painting **realistic scenes** of rural and working life, including all its harsh details. This was not approved of by the art academies, which preferred paintings about historical, religious, and mythological subjects. Courbet became an outspoken advocate of **"realism"** (he coined the phrase). His modern approach to painting was frank in style and unsentimental in expression. The Realism movement in art quickly gained momentum in Europe.

— **Painting REAL LIFE** —

In the late 1800s, Japanese woodblock prints (see page 54) were seen in Europe. Their boldness, simplicity, and unmodeled figures influenced the Impressionists. Artists were especially affected by the **lack of perspective** and shadow, as well as the flat areas of strong color.

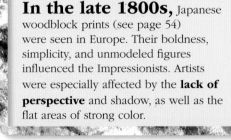

Jeanne, *1881, by Edouard Manet*

The Impressionist style originated in France, but spread to other countries...

French Impressionism

Claude Monet
Impression: Sunrise, *1873*
The name "Impressionism" was given to the new style of painting by an art critic at the group's first exhibition after seeing the name of this painting by Monet.

Edgar Degas
The Dancing Class, *c.1873-76*
After meeting the Impressionists, Degas chose scenes from real life to paint, such as ballet dancers practicing, busy café interiors, and people at work.

Alfred Sisley
Snow at Louveciennes, *1875*
Most of Sisley's work is of landscapes, painted with a light touch and with the pure colors applied unmixed onto the canvas, typical of the Impressionist style.

Pierre-Auguste Renoir
Ball at the Moulin de la Galette, *1876*
This scene of people enjoying themselves in the open air, with sunlight filtering through the trees, is typical of Renoir's work as a true Impressionist. Later, he experimented with his style, painting over 6,000 works in his lifetime.

Berthe Morisot
The Cherry Picker, *1891*
Morisot was the first woman to join the Impressionists. Her brightly colored paintings often showed women and family life.

Camille Pissarro
The Farm at Osny, *1883*
Older than most members of the Impressionist group, Pissarro was influential in teaching and guiding the other artists on painting outdoors.

Outside France

Philip Wilson Steer
Beach at Etaples, *1887*
The British artist Steer used the Impressionist style to capture the effects of light on his beach scenes and seascapes.

Tom Roberts
A Break Away! *1891*
Roberts introduced Impressionism to Australia, using the style to paint landscapes, portraits, rural life, and scenes from history.

Childe Hassam
Isle of Shoals, *1906*
An American Impressionist, Hassam spent his summers on the coast in New Hampshire and captured the lighting effects on this landscape.

Artist's biography
Claude **Monet**

1840: *Born in Paris but grew up in Le Havre, France*

1859: *At age 19 studied art at the Académie Suisse in Paris*

1861–62: *Drafted into the army and served in Algeria, Africa*

1870–71: *At age 30 lived in London with his new wife, Camille, during the Franco-Prussian War*

1873: *In Paris, he painted* Impression: Sunrise *(see page 59)*

1883: *Settled in Giverny, on the Seine, 40 miles (65 km) from Paris*

1903: *Eyesight began to fail but continued painting*

1926: *Died at age 86 and a year later a series of Waterlilies was housed in the Orangerie, Paris, and opened to the public*

Artist's influences

Johan Jongkind
—Taught Monet to look closely and clearly at the light effects in nature

Édouard Manet
—Inspired by his bold brushstrokes and scenes of modern life

Claude **Monet**

"My garden is my most beautiful masterpiece."

Monet was one of the most famous of the French Impressionist artists. All his life, he claimed that nature was his studio and his **series paintings** show his interest in capturing the changing

light. He would work on a whole series showing the same subject but at different times of the day. He would change from one canvas to another as the Sun moved across the sky, and then start again with the first canvas the next day.

Painting large

In 1916, Monet built a studio to house a number of large canvases he had begun working on. Each of these canvases was **over 14 ft (4 m) wide**. He wanted to recreate his oriental garden as a large mural.

The Waterlily Pond: Pink Harmony, *1900, Oil on canvas*
How is this painting similar to *Green Harmony*? How is it different? This one was painted in the summer.

The Japanese Bridge, *1918, Oil on canvas*
Monet's brushstrokes became broad and sweeping with strong bright colors in his later life due to his failing eyesight.

An oriental water garden

In 1893, Monet bought a plot of land across the road from his garden in Giverny. Here, he dug out a pond, planted trees and flowers, and built a **Japanese bridge** to create an oriental water garden. Over the next 25 years, he sketched and painted over 250 images of his **waterlilies,** of which a series of 10 canvases featured the bridge and pond in different lighting conditions.

One of Monet's sketches of the pond with waterlilies in purple pencil.

The Waterlily Pond: Green Harmony, *1899, 34¾ x 36½ in (88.3 x 93.1 cm)—Oil on canvas*

How to paint with **pastels**

A **pastel** is a stick of color made from powdered pigment mixed with a binder such as resin or gum. Pastel is applied directly to paper and there's no drying needed.

How to color layer

There are many effects that can be created with pastels, such as blending, cross-hatching, and scrumbling. Mary Cassatt's technique was to use color layering.

1 *A pale sketch is drawn in charcoal (or pencil) onto the paper, keeping the lines light.*

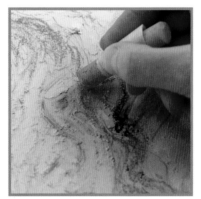

2 *Using loose, quick strokes, the first layers of pastels are applied.*

3 *The paper is sprayed with a casein fixative. This is a milky solution that stops the pastels from smudging.*

4 *Another pastel is applied using the same loose, quick strokes over the top. This effect is called color layering.*

Women Admiring a Child, *c. 1897—Pastel on paper*

Mary Cassatt's style

Mary Cassatt was an American painter who spent some of her time in France. Here, she met the **Impressionists** and during the 1880s she painted in this style to capture the fleeting moments and the effects of light. In her pastel paintings, she would apply the pastels with loose vigorous strokes, leaving soft, fuzzy edges to suggest immediacy and movement. She would **layer color** on top of color, which would make them appear as one color.

ASK YOURSELF

If you were painting a picture of a friend, what would they be wearing and what would they be holding?

Pastels timeline

Prehistoric cave paintings could be considered the first art created using dry pigments. Sticks of pastels have been used since the Renaissance.

1499 *Leonardo da Vinci experimented with yellow pastels on the dress for this preparatory chalk sketch (detail shown) for the portrait of Isabelle d'Este, a wealthy Italian lady.*

1748 *In this portrait of the French king Louis XV, Maurice-Quentin de La Tour created wonderful textures for the different materials the king's wearing.*

1771 *In the 1770s, Jean-Simeon Chardin started using pastels for portraits. He hadn't done either before, but discovered he was excellent at them.*

Cassatt's favorite subjects to paint were women and children. Women were shown reading, sewing, writing letters, having tea, and joining in family activities. Cassatt's paintings show what the lives of women and children were like at the end of the 19th century.

Pastels can be held in different ways. Dragging the edge of a pastel creates large blocks of color.

Elsie Cassatt holding a big dog, c. 1880, 25 x 20½ in (63.5 x 52.1 cm)—Pastel on paper

Late-1800s *Edgar Degas used pastels to capture the movement and light effects typical of the Impressionist style.*

c. 1880 *The American Impressionist artist Mary Cassatt used quick strokes and layering of different colored pastels to create her paintings.*

1902 *Stanislaw Wyspianski had an allergy to oil paint, so he used pastels to create his paintings of the Polish landscape and portraits.*

2007 *Daniel Greene, an award-winning artist, uses pastels for his portraits and still-life paintings, such as this one of a Green Checkerboard, Balloons, and Darts.*

Vincent van Gogh

Artist's biography
Vincent van Gogh

1853: *Born in Zundert, Netherlands*

1869: *Worked at the international picture dealers Goupil and Co. but was forced to resign after seven years*

1878: *Worked as a lay preacher among miners in Belgium*

1886: *Moved to Paris to live with his brother and met the Impressionist painters*

1888: *Settled in Arles in the south of France, hoping to start a community of artists— but he never did*

1889: *Decides to enter an asylum in nearby St. Rémy, where he painted* The Starry Night *(see page 66)*

1890: *At age 37, committed suicide*

Artist's influences

Paul Gauguin
—Influenced by the same subjects when lived and painted together in Arles

Jean-François Millet
—Influenced by Millet's respectful depiction of laborers in the fields

"I am risking my life for my work, and half my reason has gone."

At age 27, **Vincent van Gogh** taught himself to draw with only a little teaching, and continued to develop his skills throughout his life. He painted self portraits to practice his technique. He bought a mirror and painted himself—more than **30 times**.

Practice makes perfect—Self portraits

Fall 1886
Van Gogh used dark colors in his early paintings, until he met the Impressionists in Paris.

Summer 1887
Van Gogh now experimented with light, vibrant colors and practiced using short brushstrokes.

Winter 1888
Now confident with his own colorful style, he moved to Arles, hoping to create a school of art with his artist friends.

January 1889
He began to show signs of mental illness and after a violent quarrel with a close friend, Gauguin, cut off part of his ear.

Fall 1889
In an asylum, suffering from mental distress, he painted with curving, swirling lines.

Van Gogh applied the thick oil paint with fat paintbrushes or by squeezing straight out of the tube.

Imagine if you could walk into this painting...

One of van Gogh's favorite paintings was this one of his bedroom in the Yellow House at Arles, in the south of France. He painted with **dramatic colors**. In reality, his room had very little furniture. He added two chairs to represent himself and his friend Gauguin and he painted other examples of his work hanging on the walls. This was the first of three versions he painted.

An artist named Seward Johnson re-created Van Gogh's painting for an American museum. You can sit on everything.

TRY A PORTRAIT OF YOUR OWN
Position a mirror in front of you and draw your portrait and then add bold colors.

By Jason, age 10

Self-portrait in felt hat, *1887, 17¼ x 14¾ in (44 x 37.5 cm)—Oil on canvas*

Nighttime **in art**

Nighttime creates **different moods** in art. In some of these paintings there are themes of loneliness and fear, while others show much happier scenes, including dancing and celebration.

▶ **The Dance,** **1988,** **Paula Rego, Acrylic on paper** This painting is inspired by Rego's childhood in Portugal. It is also said to represent the different stages of life, showing the generations from youth to old age.

▲ **Starry Night,** **1889, Vincent van Gogh, Oil on canvas**
Van Gogh painted this piece while in a mental hospital. He rarely sold any of his paintings during his lifetime. Since his death, however, *Starry Night* has become one of the best-known paintings in modern culture.

SEEING THINGS
For more on Vincent van Gogh
see page 64

◄ **Automat,** 1927, **Edward Hopper,
Oil on canvas** Many of Hopper's paintings show
people alone, mostly in urban settings. In this
painting, a woman sits in a quiet café drinking
coffee by herself. It is night, and judging by her
coat and hat, it is also cold outside.

▲ **Carnation, Lily, Lily, Rose,**
1885–86, John Singer Sargent, Oil on canvas
Sargent was staying with friends when he decided
to paint a scene of their children lighting Japanese
lanterns at dusk on a summer evening.

◄ **Creole Dance,** before
**1927, Pedro Figari, Oil on
cardboard** The creole dance was
traditionally performed in Latin
America. Figari, an artist from Uruguay,
painted scenes from the local people's
lives, including their nighttime dancing.

▲ **Ceremony under the Moon,**
2004, Artist unknown, Oil on canvas This is a
modern painting showing a nighttime scene.

▲ **The Mail Coach in a Thunderstorm,** 1827,
James Pollard, engraved by R. G. Reeve, Color litho Pollard was known for
his scenes of horses and coaches. This is an aquatint-engraving, which uses a
metal plate covered with a special substance to create a grainy texture.

After Impressionism

Impressionism had a major impact on Western art. Artists broke away from the expectation that art should be large, formal, highly finished paintings. Instead, artists could **express their personalities** and give a response to the world through their art. After Impressionism there came a period of even more innovation, as artists pushed the boundaries even further.

La Dame aux Camelias, *1896, by Alphonse Mucha*

Art Nouveau

("New art") was a popular decorative, though short-lived, movement that first appeared in the 1890s and was inspired by floral and **stylized, curvy motifs**. Alphonse Mucha, a Czech artist, became famous in 1895 when he produced a poster of the popular Parisian actress Sarah Bernhardt that embraced this style of art.

Art Nouveau

Fauvism

Expressionism

Symbolism

Neo-Impressionism

Postimpressionism

Card Players, *c. 1890-92, by Paul Cézanne*

Sunday Afternoon on the Island of La Grand Jatte, *c. 1884-86, by Georges Seurat*

Upa upa (Tahitian Fire Dance), *c. 1891, by Paul Gauguin*

Postimpressionism

describes the development of French art from the mid1880s through to the early 20th century. Artists such as Paul Cézanne wanted to develop, but also **challenge**, the ideals of Impressionism. Cézanne hoped to bring more of a **sense of order** to his work, structuring it more tightly.

Neo-Impressionism

was a term used to describe the work of Georges Seurat and Paul Signac in the 1880s. They experimented with using small dots to build up an artwork (because of this the style is also known as **Pointillism**). Seurat's most famous painting, *Sunday Afternoon on the Island of La Grande Jatte*, was completed in 1886.

Symbolism

emerged in the late 1800s, largely as a reaction against Realism and Impressionism. The movement saw artists explorir the realms of **fantasy** and using metaphors in their works to suggest their own ideas of **mystery** Some, for example, used the Bible, while others used spirits or ghosts. Paul Gauguin spent part of his life in Tahiti, where he gained inspiration for his painting *Upa upa (Tahitian Fire Dance)*.

Elasticity, 1916,
by Umberto Boccioni

Conference at Night,
1949, by Edward Hopper

Bridge on the Thames,
c. 1905, by André Derain

Fauvism looked to a **vivid use of color** and was an art movement led by close friends Henri Matisse and André Derain, who were termed *Les Fauves* ("the wild beasts") in 1905 by a critic. Fauvist brushwork was bold and the subject was simplified. Derain depicted London in a new colorful way using bright colour, and short, broken brushmarks.

Futurism appeared in Italy in the early 20th century. It looked to the triumph of **technology** and invention over nature and toward a promising future rather than dwelling on the past. The **swirling, fractured shapes** and forms in Umberto Boccioni's works show his love of speed and technology.

Realism took daily life as its subject-matter and aimed to depict it as **realistically** as possible. It began in France in the 1850s. Later, an American artist, Edward Hopper, became a leading example of this kind of art, making arresting images of ordinary life in America.

The Scream,
1893, by Edvard Munch

The Syphon, *20th century, by Emilio Pettoruti*

Locomotive Construction, *1930, by Joaquín Torres García*

Expressionism twists and distorts reality in art, with the goal of provoking an emotional response in the viewer. It could often be an expression of an artist's **inner turmoil** and confusion. Edvard Munch showed this to great effect in his painting *The Scream.*

Cubism was a revolutionary new form of painting, seen famously in the work of Pablo Picasso, that emerged in 1907 and lasted into the early 1920s. Subjects of Cubist paintings are **broken up** and painted as if viewed from different angles. Emilio Pettoruti was an Argentinian painter who experimented with Cubism and whose exhibition of Cubist work in 1924 in Argentina was considered very shocking.

Constructivism grew after 1921 following dramatic changes in the political structure within Russia. Art came to be seen as a tool that could embrace **social change** and inspire future development. It inspired artists outside Russia as well, one being Joaquín Torres García, a Uruguayan artist.

Henri Matisse

"When I paint green, it doesn't mean grass; when I paint blue, it doesn't mean sky."

Artist's biography
Henri **Matisse**

1869: *Born in northeastern France*

1887: *Went to Paris to study law, became ill, and turned to studying art in 1891*

1904-1907: *Became the leader of a group of avant-garde artists called the Fauves (wild beasts)*

1908: *Published* Notes of a Painter, *describing his theory about painting*

1921: *Moved to the south of France*

1941: *Became confined to bed or a wheelchair after two operations*

1954: *Died of a heart attack at 85*

When he was recovering from an illness at the age of 20, Matisse was given a box of paints by his mother. This moment began his career as an artist. Matisse was obsessed with **color** and used it to create shapes, mood, and emotion. He played and experimented with color all his life, often creating the feelings of joy and **playfulness** in his works.

Artist's influences

Three Bathers* by Paul Cezanne—Bought in 1899, influenced layout of paintings*

Islamic art—*Influenced by the use of patterns and the decorative use of color*

Drawing with scissors

Cutting out paper, arranging the pieces into a picture, and pasting them onto a flat surface is a technique known as **collage**. When Matisse was no longer able to stand or see well, he chose to use this technique. With the help of assistants, he painted sheets of paper, **cut out different shapes**, and then arranged and pasted them down.

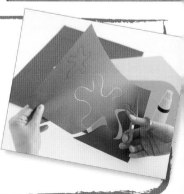

NOW YOU TRY...

Try creating your own picture in the style of Matisse.

Like Matisse, you can be creative with colored paper. Paint pieces of paper in bright colors and then cut them into shapes. Move the shapes around until you're happy with their arrangement.

The Sorrows of the King, *1952, 115 x 152 in (292 x 386 cm)—*
Gouache on paper on canvas

Colors and patterns stand out in Matisse's pictures. How many colors can you find in this picture? How do the colors make you feel? Matisse chose his colors to **express emotions** and cleverly arranged them so that the picture is relaxing to look at. In his picture of a snail, he arranged the shapes in a spiral to suggest the shell.

The Snail, *1953, Gouache on paper on canvas*

Cut out clues

In addition to color, Matisse understood body shapes and he could suggest an object or person by showing a simplified shape with a few **flowing lines**. In this picture, can you find the sorrowful king playing his guitar, and a dancer and a seated figure trying to cheer him up.

71

Artist's biography
Pablo **Picasso**

1881: *Born in Malaga, southern Spain*

1901: *At age 20 visited Paris and painted pictures of destitute street figures in shades of blue, known as his "Blue Period"*

1904: *Settled in Paris. Painted circus figures and harlequins in orange and pink colors, known as his "Rose Period"*

1907: *At age 26, painted* Les Demoiselles d'Avignon, *which broke with the traditions of Western art*

1909–1914: *Worked with Georges Braque to find new ways of showing space and volume—now called Cubism*

1946-1973: *Lived in the south of France, continuing his painting and experimenting with ceramics until his death*

Artist's influences

Paul Cezanne—*Inspired by looking at the shape and form of nature*

African sculpture —*Inspired by the boldness and expressiveness of these non-Western works*

Pablo **Picasso**

"When you come down to it, all you have is yourself."

The Spanish artist Picasso was a **gifted artist** even as a child and became one of the most important modern artists. He was bold, original, and inventive, and used all kinds of art materials, including collage and ceramics. The themes he chose were often about himself and also **universal**: love, violence, birth, and death.

Model and muse

The woman in the photograph and seated in the chair is the French photographer **Dora Maar**, who was Picasso's mistress and muse (inspiration) for seven years. Beautiful, intelligent, and politically aware, she took step-by-step photographs of Picasso painting *Guernica*.

This photograph shows Dora in about 1947.

This portrait shows Dora from two different angles—in profile and full face.

Guernica

During the **Spanish Civil War**, the small town of Guernica in Spain was attacked by 28 bombers on April 26, 1937. Immediately afterward, Picasso painted this large picture. He wanted to show the **suffering** of ordinary people and animals and to bring the civil war in Spain to everyone's attention.

Guernica *1937, Oil on canvas*

Study of a weeping woman

This painting of a woman mourning was used as a study for *Guernica* (below). Picasso used Dora's features. He wanted to show the woman's suffering and to do this he **distorted** her face and used colors in an expressive, not a naturalistic, way.

Look closer
Look at all the jagged lines in the painting and how they convey the quality of grief. We can actually feel someone crying. Picasso has combined the folds of a handkerchief with the fingers and made the fingernails look like tears.

The pupil in Dora's eye looks almost like a military plane, to symbolize the ones that attacked Guernica.

Did you know that
Picasso and his friend Georges Braque developed a new art style called **Cubism**? The surface of the painting was fragmented, altering shapes and showing different viewpoints at the same time.

Weeping Woman, *1937, 33¼ x 29 in (84.7 x 73.9 cm)—Oil on canvas*

Naïve art

Naïve painting is the work of artists with little or no formal art training. In the 20th century, these simple almost cartoonlike paintings with their **bright colors** and awkward drawing became popular and even inspired the work of other artists. The naïve artists were interested in the **subject matter** and often chose to paint their favorite subjects.

Grandma Moses
Come on Old Topsy, *20th century*
An American farmer's wife, Anna Moses only started painting in her 70s. Over the next 30 years (she died at age 101), she produced an amazing 3,600 paintings, mostly about her memories of farm life.

Henri Rousseau
Jungle with Horse Attacked by a Jaguar, *1910*
The French self-taught artist Rousseau is best known for painting wild animals in tropical jungle scenes, but these were fantasy. He had never seen a jungle, but just studied tropical plants in the botanical garden in Paris for reference.

Alfred Wallis **Two Boats with Yellow Sails and Lighthouse,** *20th century*
Wallis, a British fisherman and scrap merchant, only began painting in his 60s. His main subjects were ships, fishing, and coastal villages.

Camille Bombois
The Itinerant Athlete, *c.1930*
The French naïve artist Bombois is famous for painting circus scenes. In his youth, he was a champion local wrestler and then joined a traveling circus as a strongman.

Wilson Bigaud
Bal Militaire, *20th century*
Bigaud, one of the naïve artists from Haiti, featured scenes of everyday life in his country, including lively carnivals and dances. In this painting and many others, he bathed the scenes in golden light.

Dora Holzhandler
Ice Cream Parlor, Bude, *2008*
Holzhandler loved patterns and often her pictures featured stripes and checks on the characters' clothes, and on furniture and wallpaper.

Ivan Rabuzin
My World, *1962*
A Croatian carpenter, Rabuzin developed an interest in painting in his 20s and painted whenever he had the time. His first exhibition of paintings when he was 35 was so successful that he later gave up his job and became a full-time painter. He continued to learn about art by visiting galleries and reading about various artists.

Beryl Cook
Granny the Lion Tamer, *1983*
Cook started painting in her 40s when she borrowed a paint-box from her son. This British artist is famous for painting funny pictures of "fat ladies."

Laurence Stephen Lowry
After the Wedding, *1939*
The British artist Lowry was one of a number of trained painters who adopted the style of naïve art. His urban scenes usually featured factories and other grimy buildings against a white sky and crowds of stylized, spindly figures, known as "matchstick men."

Artist's biography
Paul **Klee**

1879: *Born near Berne in Switzerland*

1898: *At 19 years old, moved to Munich to study at the Academy of Fine Art*

1901-02: *Toured Rome, Naples, and Florence in Italy*

1911: *Joined a group of artists in Germany called Der Blaue Reiter (The Blue Rider)*

1912: *At age 33 visited Paris, met Delaunay and was influenced by Cubism*

1920-31: *Painted and taught at the Bauhaus School of Art and Design in Weimar in Germany*

1933: *Returned to Switzerland to escape Nazi persecution*

1940: *Died in Switzerland*

Artist's influences

Franz Marc—*Inspired by the use of very bold colors for expression*

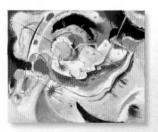

Wassily Kandinsky —*Inspired by the fresh and free way Kandinsky used color*

Paul **Klee**

"I want to be as though newborn... almost primitive."

Castle and Sun, *1928, 19¾ x 23¼ in (50 x 59 cm)—Oil on canvas*

A hugely original and now popular artist, Paul Klee was also amazingly productive. By the time he died, he had produced more than **9,000 works.** His style is hard to pin down—some of his images are straightforward and **figurative,** while others are completely abstract.

Senecio, *1922, Oil on primed gauze on cardboard*

Assorted shapes

Strongly influenced by Cubism, this abstracted portrait (*Senecio* means "old man") is drawn in soft colors and **geometric shapes**. A simple triangle suggests the disapproving raised eyebrow that reflects Klee's sharp wit.

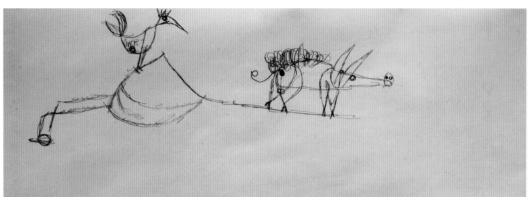

Cock and pig, *1920, Pen on paper*

"A drawing is simply a line going for a walk."

Taking a line for a walk

This is the way Klee thought of drawing. He would start to **doodle** with a pencil, see what shapes appeared, then play with what he saw. Like a child, Klee relied heavily on his **imagination**, finding endless inspiration by experimenting with colors and shapes as well as pencil lines.

Painting music

Paul Klee was a talented musician, and he trained as a violinist. This passion comes through in his pictures, where he often arranges blocks of color like notes in a **melody**, set off with harmonizing shades as in a musical composition. *Castle and Sun*, although it consists only of shapes and colors, is so carefully constructed that it clearly portrays rows of buildings. Klee's main passion was for **color**: "Color and I are one," he wrote.

NOW YOU TRY...

Try to draw your own picture in the style of Klee.

Try painting simple figures set off by lines, squares, rectangles, circles, and triangles in really bright colors. Use your box of watercolor paints—when Klee was a young painter, he always worked in watercolors.

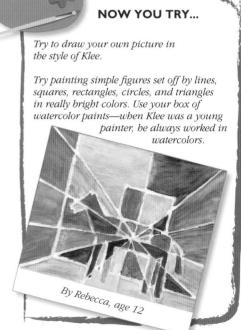

By Rebecca, age 12

Surrealism

Surreal means **"more than real"**: Surrealist painters thought that powerful feelings could be expressed through **dreamlike** paintings where ordinary objects were shown in impossible situations. This questioning of reality was in response to the horrors of World War I.

In the late **1800s**, there was renewed interest in the work of some **16th century artists**, such as **Hieronymus Bosch** and **Guiseppe Arcimboldo**, who had painted imaginary worlds and experimented with unusual ideas.

Hieronymus Bosch
Bosch's oil paintings were visions crammed with weird creatures and distorted figures.

The Garden of Earthly Delights (detail), c. 1500

Hieronymus BOSCH (c. 1450–1516)

Guiseppe Arcimboldo
As a **Renaissance** artist, **Arcimboldo** was ahead of his time. His detailed paintings showed flowers, fruits, and vegetables arranged as fantastic heads.

Spring, 16th century

Guiseppe ARCIMBOLDO (c. 1527–1593)

James Ensor
In the late **19th century,** the Belgian artist **Ensor** became known for his fantasy paintings, featuring carnival figures and masks, puppets, and skeletons.

Old Woman with Masks, 1889

James ENSOR (1860–1949)

Nude Descending a Staircase, No.2, 1912, by Marcel Duchamp

From **1906, color photography** became available, along with other developments in photographic techniques. Artists were inspired to **mimic** these techniques, such as images taken in quick succession.

Photographic DEVELOPMENTS

Weeping Woman, 1937, by Pablo Picasso

Cubist paintings showed a subject fragmented from many viewpoints. Art had become a way of **expressing opinions.**

1914–1918
The destruction and suffering of **World War I** was blamed on the upper class's control over society.

The Anguish of Departure, 1913–4

From **1910** and into the **1920s,** the Italian artist **Chirico** painted **dreamlike** pictures of unrelated objects in deserted places, including unidentifiable figures and strange shadows.

Giorgio de CHIRICO (1888–1978)

CUBISM

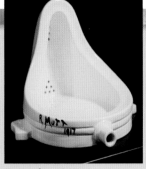

Fountain, 1917,
by Marcel Duchamp

While the rest of Europe was at war, the **Dada movement** began in Switzerland—so-called after a baby's first sounds. The artists protested against the **foolishness of war** by sticking together fragments of everyday objects to make supposedly meaningless art. **Marcel Duchamp** used "ready-made" mass-produced objects to show the **absurdity** of life.

DADA

1924
The French poet and critic **Andre Breton** started the idea of **Surrealism** based on the psychologist **Sigmund Freud's** work on dreams and the **unconscious mind**. Surrealist writers wrote whatever thoughts they had as quickly as possible.

The mind is like an iceburg, it floats with one-seventh of its bulk above water.

Sigmund Freud (1856–1939)

Surrealist artists tried different ways to reveal their unconscious thoughts...

Automatism

Max Ernst
Massacre of the Innocents, *1921*
Ernst created Surrealist collages by putting together a random collection of images from catalogs, textbooks, and advertisements. This uncontrolled process was called visual automatism.

Andre Masson
Automatic Drawing, *c.1924-25*
Seriously wounded in WWI, Masson suffered from nightmares and fits of rage. He would spontaneously draw when he was stressed, sometimes after purposely not eating or drinking for a long time.

ANOTHER DIRECTION

Man Ray
Rayograph (gyroscope, magnifying glass, pin), *1922*
Man Ray placed everyday objects on photographic light-sensitive paper and exposed them to light, making the objects' flat shapes and shadows appear on the paper. This was called a rayograph.

Dreamlike

Salvador Dali
**Premonition of Civil War:
Soft Construction with Boiled Beans,** *1936*
Spanish artist Dali made strange dreamlike paintings by looking intensely at a set of objects until he could see others, like a hallucination.

Yves Tanguy
Through Birds Through Fire But Not Through Glass, *1943*
On his strange ocean or Moon-like landscapes, Tanguy used nongeometric shapes to suggest living things, a method called biomorphism.

Rene Magritte
The Liberator, *1947*
Magritte painted familiar objects, animals, and people in scenes that didn't make sense. He repeated some objects in other paintings.

Artist's biography
Joan **Miró**

1893: *Born in Barcelona, Spain*

1919: *At age 26 visited Paris for the first time and continued to spend winters there until the start of the Spanish Civil War in 1936, when he settled there*

1940: *Returned to Spain to escape the German occupation of France, settling mainly on the island of Majorca*

1947: *Visited the United States for the first time to produce a mural*

1958: *Installed two huge ceramic wall decorations in the UNESCO building, Paris*

1983: *Died in Majorca*

Artist's influences

Pablo Picasso
—*Inspired by Cubist idea of showing many viewpoints*

Francis Picabia
—*Inspired by Dada idea of scattered and random forms*

Joan **Miró**

The Spanish artist **Joan Miró** used his memory and imagination to paint his pictures. One of his happy memories was of the many **Falles**, Spanish festivals that he had taken part in when he was young. In 1925, while in Paris, Miró painted **The Carnival of the Harlequin** by letting his subconscious mind make the images—a method a bit like doodling.

The Falles was a parade of huge colorful puppets made from papier-mâché called fallas, which were then burned on the final day of the two-week festival.

In 1956, Miró moved to a house in Majorca, where he lived until his death in 1983. His studio was filled with his **fantasy paintings** and sculptures. Black stains of paint can still be seen on the floor.

Flowing lines, curved objects, and twisted shapes were features of Miró's style. He used a handful of bright colors against a plain background.

A harlequin is a clownlike figure. Can you find him in the painting? What do you think he is feeling? A harlequin costume is usually split into areas of contrasting primary colors.

Carnival of the Harlequin, *1924-5,*
26 x 36½ in (66 x 93 cm)—Oil on canvas

What can you see in Miró's surreal
(dreamlike) painting called the **Carnival
of the Harlequin**? Can you recognize
animals, objects, and shapes? Why are
they scattered in a room? Maybe it's
Miró's mind or perhaps a workshop.

NOW YOU TRY...

*Try drawing your own picture in
the style of Miró.*

*Think of a favorite memory,
perhaps a party or a circus.
Draw some of the images you
can remember in a curved,
twisted way and use lots of
bright colors.*

Mark Grady, age 10

Grant **Wood**

" All the good ideas I've ever had came to me while I was milking a cow."

1891: *Born on a farm near Anamosa, Iowa*

1901: *At age 10, left the farm with his mother after his father's death and moved to Cedar Rapids*

1913: *Enrolled in the School of the Art Institute of Chicago*

1914: *At age 23 joined the army during WWI and painted camouflage on tanks and cannons*

1920: *Made the first of several trips to Europe to study Impressionist and Postimpressionist art*

1930: *Painted his most famous work, American Gothic*

1934: *At age 43 appointed assistant professor of fine art at University of Iowa*

1942: *Died of liver cancer in Iowa City*

Artist's influences

Northern masters
*—Inspired by the realism of Netherlandish masters such as Hans Memling (*Portrait of a Man, *c. 1485, detail above)*

 American Gothic, *1930, 29¼ × 24½ in (74.3 × 62.4 cm)—Oil on beaverboard (compressed wood pulp used for construction)*

Grant Wood was a painter from the American Midwest who captured the **ordinary people** and scenes he grew up with. While abstract and other kinds of modern art were fashionable in Europe, Wood's truthful style and simple **country subject matter** offered a complete contrast. His style became known as **Regionalism**.

The farmhouse in the picture is still standing in Eldon, Iowa.

Pointed in the medieval Gothic architectural style, this arched window inspired the painting's name.

Some experts think Wood deliberately used repeated patterns of three lines or shapes in his picture. This window has three parts— can you find any other threes? (Clue: look at the pitchfork, the man's overalls, and the deep wrinkles below his glasses.)

American symbol

Possibly the most familiar American painting of all time, *American Gothic* was inspired by a house with an **unusual window** (above). Wood added "the kind of people I fancied should live in that house." The woman who posed for him was his sister Nan, and the man was his dentist. Do you think this couple are husband and wife, or father and daughter? Are they grumpy and rigid, or dignified and serious?

Life on the prairies

In the winter of 1932–1933, the US's economy was at the lowest point of the **Great Depression**, which had begun in 1929 when the stock market crashed. Many people were unemployed and agriculture, mining, and other industries in America were struggling. Wood painted **hopeful pictures** showing good times. *Dinner for Threshers* shows a scene from the 19th century, when there was no machinery and agriculture was thriving.

During the early 1930s, American farmlands became a dry dust bowl, yet Wood portrayed these fields as a fertile, appealingly rounded landscape. People are drawn to Wood's pictures because they are warm and friendly.

Stone City, Iowa, *1930, Oil on panel*

Dinner for Threshers, *1934, Oil on hardboard*

Animals in art

Animals have featured in art since the first markings on **cave walls** thousands of years ago. The varied styles of art have shown **different aspects** of animals from adored pets to powerful beasts to incarnations of spiritual gods.

▶ **Development II,** 1939, M. C. Escher, **Woodcut printed from three blocks** Many of Escher's works used repeated tiled patterns called tessellations. In this picture, he was thinking about infinity gradually reducing the reptiles into tiny hexagons.

SEEING THINGS
For more on African sculpture see page 112

◀ **Horse and train,** 1954, Alex Colville, **Glazed oil on hardboard** Inspired by a World War I poem, Colville wanted to show that although a situation may seem hopeless, choices can be made. Will the train stop or the horse leave the tracks to avoid a collision?

◀ **Woman on horseback,** late 18th century, **Kim Hong-do, Ink and light color on paper** Kim Hong-do was a great Korean court painter of the late 18th century who painted the daily activities of people.

◀ **Buffalo mask,** Bamileke tribe, Wood In Cameroon, masks were worn at tribal ceremonies. Buffalos were considered powerful and brave and these masks, with glaring almond-shaped eyes and large teeth and nostrils, symbolized the power of the chief.

▲ **Luminous Char,** 2008, **Kenojuak Ashevak, Stonecut and stencil** Born in an igloo in 1927, the Canadian artist Ashevak combined her native traditional Inuit culture with Western art styles in her work.

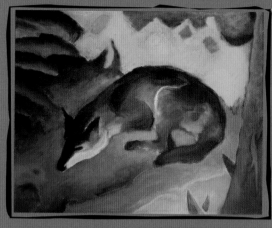

▶ Blue Fox, 1911,
Franz Marc, Oil on canvas
The Expressionist painter Franz Marc painted his animals in symbolic colors to convey their spiritual nature. He used blue for masculinity, yellow for joy and happiness, and red for motherhood. For Marc, blue was the most deeply spiritual primary color.

◀ Puppy,
1992, Jeff Koons, Stainless steel, soil, geotextile fabric, flowering plants This 43-ft (12.4-m) high sculpture of a West Highland White Terrier puppy now stands outside the Guggenheim Museum in Bilbao, Spain. The steel structure is covered in a variety of living flowers with an internal watering system.

▲ A Monkey, 1500s, Albrecht
Durer, Watercolor and gouache on paper
The Renaissance painter and engraver Albrecht Durer was fascinated by animals and was one of the first artists to show animals as subjects on their own.

▲ Tiger in a Tropical Storm
(Surprised), 1891, Henri Rousseau, Oil
on canvas The self-taught French artist Rousseau painted wild animals in jungle landscapes based on his visits to the Botanical Gardens in Paris.

▲ Horses, 1950, Xu Beihong,
Chinese ink and color on paper
The Chinese artist, Xu Beihong, was known for his horse paintings. His inkwork captured the spirited movement of the horses.

Postwar abstract art

How did it happen?

In the 20th century a new style was created, where artists made up their own shapes and colors to express their emotions. In these **abstract** paintings, people, places, or objects were unrecognizable. This new style was used by artists in many different movements. After World War II (1939-1945), artists used abstract art to convey their innermost feelings.

Impressionist—Edgar Degas
- 19th century -

Movements of the late 19th century (**Impressionism, Neo-Impressionism and Postimpressionism**) stressed the importance of the **creative process** as well as the subject.

Movements of the early 20th century (**Symbolism, Fauvism, and Expressionism**) used color to express strong **personal emotions.**

Expressionist—Edvard Munch
- 20th century -

Improvisation 9, 1910, Oil on canvas

Kandinsky is considered the **founder** of abstract art, having founded the movement in the 1920s. He was inspired after seeing an upside-down painting and liking the shapes and colors.

Wassily KANDINSKY (1866-1944)

Suprematist Construction, 1910, Oil on board

Malevich's suprematist art has been described as hard-edged and minimal. To him, a square represented spiritual perfection.

Kasimir MALEVICH (1878-1935)

Composition with Red, Blue, and Yellow, 1930, Oil on canvas

Mondrian's art used **geometric shapes**. To him, these shapes freed him from his subject so he could achieve a spiritual state.

Piet MONDRIAN (1872-1944)

Surrealists during the 1930s painted in a dreamlike state to reveal **unconscious feelings.**

1940s SOCIETY

Surrealist—Salvador Dalí
- 1930s -

Postwar society of the late 1940s was being entertained by the **new technology** of the radio, movies, and television. **Abstract artists** wanted to also find new ways of painting.

Then postwar abstract artists went in different directions...

Color field

Helen Frankenthaler
Great Meadows, *1951*
Frankenthaler devised a soak-stain technique, using very diluted oil and acrylic paint, so the painting would have no brushstrokes or surface texture.

Mark Rothko
Untitled, *1960-61*
Rothko often conveyed quiet, thoughtful emotion through large spaces of a single color. His huge canvases convey a feeling of isolation in a world with no end.

ANOTHER DIRECTION

Fahrelnissa Zeid
Pochoir stencil, plate XXIX
Témoignages pour l'art abstrait, *1952*
Zeid was a Turkish princess who combined abstract art with inspirations from Islamic and Byzantine art. She described herself as painting in a trance, losing herself within the painting.

Action

Willem de Kooning
Door to the River, *1960*
De Kooning and Jackson Pollock (see page 88) were called Action painters. For them, the "act" of painting becomes the subject of the work, revealing their dramatic emotions.

Franz Kline
New York, N.Y., *1953*
Kline started out as a realistic painter but then for a while—in the late 1940s and 1950s—painted large abstract black-and-white calligraphic paintings of his observations.

Paul-Émile Borduas
Autumn reception, *1953*
The radical Canadian abstract painter Borduas tried to paint "automatically," without any thought beforehand of what he was going to do.

Geometric

Maria Helena Vieira da Silva
Echec et Mat, *1949*
The paintings of the Portugese abstract artist Vieira da Silva are full of detail and complex shapes and forms to convey her search for the never-ending truth.

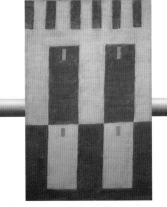

Alfredo Volpi
Façade in Blue, White and Pink, *1950*
Volpi taught himself to paint. He is famous for painting abstracts of the colorful, small flags from Brazilian folklore used in the annual June festival.

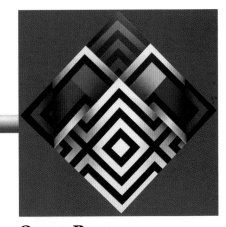

Omar Rayo
Mateo's Toy, *2009*
Rayo is a Colombian graphic artist famous for his abstract geometric paintings. He uses squares, rectangles, and zigzags in black, white, and sometimes red colors.

Jackson Pollock

"When I am in my painting, I have a general notion of what I am about."

Artist's biography
Jackson **Pollock**

1912: *Born in Cody, Wyoming, and grew up in Arizona and California*

1930: *At age 18, moved to New York City to study art with the mural painter Thomas Hart Benton*

1936: *Worked with Mexican muralists and was introduced to the effects of paint being poured at an experimental workshop*

1945: *Married the painter Lee Krasner*

1947–52: *During this time, created his most famous "drip" paintings*

1956: *At the age of 44, died in a car accident*

Artist's influences

Native Indian sand painting
—Inspired by the way different colored sands were trickled to form symbolic images

Jackson Pollock is a famous **abstract expressionist** painter because he created a whole new way of painting. In 1947, he suddenly stopped standing at easels and using palettes and brushes and started dripping household paint over huge canvases on the floor. Nobody had painted like this before: the artist's way of working with paint and the canvas was made the subject of the painting. These **action paintings** became very popular.

Number 1, *1948, 5 ft 8 in x 8 ft 8 in (172.7 x 264.2 cm)*
—Oil and enamel on unprimed canvas

Drip and splash

Pollock created his **"drip" paintings** by nailing a large canvas to the floor and then moving around it while pouring, dripping, and flinging paint. These movements were **energetic** and emotional yet controlled. The paintings have no main focus and all parts of the picture are equally important.

Pollock's signature became part of his pictures. His name would be created by dripping paint and he would also use his hands to mark the canvas. Can you find these in the painting above?

Sir Sidney **Nolan**

Artist's biography
Sir Sidney **Nolan**

1917: *Born in Melbourne, Australia*

1933: *At age 16, started working in a commercial art company*

1934: *Attended night school at the National Gallery of Victoria Art School in Melbourne*

1941-45: *At age 25, drafted into the Australian army, but went absent without leave*

1945: *Traveled through Ned Kelly country and started painting the first Ned Kelly series*

1950-51: *Traveled to Europe and settled in the United Kingdom*

1981: *Knighted for his services to art*

1992: *Died in London, UK*

Sir Sidney Nolan was an **imaginative** and expressive painter and one of the most famous Australian artists. In his paintings, he captured the bright light of the rugged Australian bush, using this as the setting for some of the most **dramatic stories** about Australian heroes. The life of Ned Kelly, a famous 19th-century outlaw, inspired Nolan to make several series of paintings.

Artist's influences

Central Australia
—*Inspired by the brilliant light*

Henri Rousseau
—*Inspired by naïve art and children's art*

 Death of Constable Scanlon, *1946, 35½ x 47¾ in (90.4 x 121.2 cm)*
Enamel on composition board

"The desire to paint the landscape involves a wish to hear more of the stories that take place in the landscape."

Nolan worked quickly, sometimes squeezing the paint straight from the tube and onto the canvas. He had his own style, often painting people, trees, and animals in a simplified way and using colors that best re-created the Australian landscape.

Ned Kelly can be recognized in Nolan's paintings by the distinctive black helmet and homemade armor. Kelly and his gang wore this armor in their gunfights with police.

The Ned Kelly series

Ned Kelly was a **bushranger** who became a folk hero for his daring and stand against the police. In 1878, as **outlaws**, he and his gang killed some police, including Constable Scanlon, at their camp at Stringybark Creek. In 1945, Nolan began his series of paintings about the events of Ned Kelly's life and returned to this subject again and again. Nolan considered himself to be an outlaw, since he had deserted from the army, and he often painted on the themes of **betrayal** and injustice.

Kelly's armor was made from parts of plows, pieces of leather, and iron bolts.

Glenrowan, *1955, Ripolin on board*

Glenrowan was the village where Kelly and his gang took their **last stand**. Police surrounded the inn where they had taken hostages and, at dawn, Kelly came out wearing his armor and marched toward the police firing his gun.

The Trial, *1947, Enamel on board*

Kelly was wounded in the legs, since his armor did not cover them, and taken to Melbourne to be **tried for murder**. He was found guilty and hanged at Old Melbourne Jail in 1880.

SEEING THINGS
For more on Pop art see page 94

▶ **Whaam!,** 1963, **Roy Lichtenstein, Acrylic and oil on canvas** Lichtenstein is famous for his cartoon-like art style. A fighter aircraft shoots a rocket at the enemy and the word Whaam! adds to the drama of the impact.

War in art

War is shown in different ways in art. Some artists paint the exact details, others portray the pain and **suffering**, while others focus on the action, such as Lichtenstein's *Whaam!*. Will a painting **glamorize** the heroics or make the viewer face the brutal reality?

▲ **Paths of Glory,** 1917, **Christopher Richard Wynne Nevinson, Oil on canvas** Nevinson worked as a Red Cross ambulance driver at the start of World War I and afterward painted what he had seen at the front lines in France.

◀ **Old Couple,** 1932, **Kathe Kollwitz, Pencil on paper** Many of Kollwitz's drawings show the suffering and grief of the people living in the very poor areas of Berlin in Germany during and after World War I.

▲ **The Triumph of War,** 1966, **Renato Guttuso, Oil on canvas** Guttuso was friends with Pablo Picasso and has included the horses from Picasso's painting *Guernica* (see page 72) in this painting.

▼ Barricade in the Rue de la Mortellerie, June 1848 (Memory of Civil War), 1849, Ernest Meissonier, Oil on canvas

Meissonier was known for his realistic observation in his art. In this painting, he shows the dead bodies of the workers who were rioting in Paris in June 1848.

▲ Allegory of War, 1690–1700, Luca Giordano, Oil on canvas

The 17th century Italian painter Giordano was admired for his many religious and mythical paintings. Even in this painting about war, a mythical god (possibly Vulcan, the Roman god who made armor and weapons in his forge) can be seen.

▲ The Kiska Patrol, 1945, E. J. Hughes, Oil on canvas

Hughes worked as an official war artist between 1940 and 1946 for his country, Canada. This painting shows Canadian soldiers patrolling the icy, mountainous island of Kiska in 1943.

▶ World War Two Pilots Scramble (detail), unveiled 2005, Paul Day, Bronze

Created for a monument about The Battle of Britain of World War II, "Scramble" was the signal for action.

Artist's biography
Andy **Warhol**

1928: *Born in Pittsburgh, Pennsylvania, the son of Slovakian immigrants*

1945: *At age 17, studied commercial art at the Carnegie Institute of Technology*

1949: *Moved to New York and began a successful career in magazine illustration*

1956: *At age 28, first group show at the Museum of Modern Art*

1962: *Founded his studio called "The Factory" and gathered a group of eccentric followers*

1962: *Developed the technique of silk-screening images directly onto canvas*

1968: *Shot and badly injured by a disgruntled member of The Factory*

1987: *At age 59, died after complications from a routine operation*

Artist's influences

Byzantine icons —*Influenced by the gold and sacredness of the images, which he saw as a child in his Roman Catholic church*

Andy **Warhol**

"Being good in business is the most fascinating kind of art."

Andy Warhol was the most famous artist of the **Pop art movement** in the US, which used images taken from the mass media, such as advertising and television. His best work was done in the 1960s when, among other things, he created portraits of **movie stars**. These explored the glamour of fame and beauty and the passing of time. Warhol challenged existing ideas about what is art and blurred the lines between fine art and popular culture.

 Marilyn, *1967, 36 x 36 in (91.5 x 91.5 cm)—Screenprint*

Movie stars in print

"Everyone will be famous for 15 minutes."

Marilyn Monroe was a very famous Hollywood movie star from the late 1940s to the early 1960s. She became an icon of beauty and glamour. However, she had emotional problems, and died of a sleeping pill overdose on August 4, 1962.

Founded in 1869, Campbell's soup is a brand recognizable around the world.

Campbell's Soup 1: Tomato, *1968, Screenprint*

After Marilyn Monroe died, Warhol used a movie publicity photograph of her and made more than **20 silkscreen paintings** of the image. Warhol used the bright colors used in advertising and made each print slightly different. The **simplified image** staring out of the picture, just like a Byzantine icon, shows no sense of the real person but only the fame and glamour. Warhol used the same technique for painting other celebrities, such as Elvis Presley and Liza Minelli.

Pop art

Inspired by advertising, packaging, and images from television and the movies, Warhol chose very **familiar objects** and celebrities as the subjects for his art. He used **advertising images**, such as soup cans, soda bottles, and boxes of cleaning products, and repeated them just as if they had been mass-produced.

Marilyn, *1967, Screenprints*

Warhol at work

Warhol called his studio "The Factory" because he was **mass-producing** his pictures. However, unlike the machine-made prints for posters and advertisements, everything he and his assistants worked on was printed by hand, making them **unique**.

NOW YOU TRY...

Try and create your own picture in the style of Warhol.

Take a digital photograph of yourself. On a computer, alter the photograph by changing the settings, lighting, colors, and filters to create a number of eye-catching images and print them out.

By Oscar aged 9

95

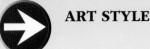

Street art

Displaying a work of art in a **public place** allows an artist to reach a very wide audience—many more people will see it than would see a painting in a gallery. But because street artists often paint their pieces on walls and buildings illegally, this type of art is often **controversial**. Some people see it as valuable art, others as simply vandalism. What do you think?

Walls of wonder

BANKSY is the most famous British street artist, but he keeps his identity a closely guarded secret. His witty and subversive works have appeared overnight in cities around the world.

PATRIES VAN ELSEN painted this colorful house in Amsterdam, Netherlands, in 1999. The mural called *The Rainbow Serpent* is found on Spuistraat Street, which has many painted houses.

This graffiti art was created by a young girl from England, who calls herself "Solveig."

Making their mark

Most street artists create their pieces with **aerosol spray paint** or marker pens. Some, such as Banksy, use a **stencil** to help produce the image quickly, which is important if the artist does not want to be caught.

Mirko Reisser (DAIM) is a 3-D graffiti artist from Germany who specializes in making his artwork appear to float above the surface of the wall. He is internationally sought after to paint street art around the world. This piece is called "auf der Lauer" (on the scout) and was spray-painted onto a wall at Kampnagel halle K3, Hamburg, Germany, in April 2005.

A name or identifying symbol sprayed on to a wall or train is known as a **tag**.

KEITH HARING was an American artist who became famous for his chalk drawings in the New York subway. This mural, called Tuttomondo, is typical of his later style, which featured bold lines and vivid colors.

MACLAIM are a trio of artists who together make superrealistic works of street art. This piece was created for an international graffiti competition, held annually in Gran Canaria, Spain, where a whole town became a canvas.

ESCIF is a Spanish street artist who often paints characters within a scene, encouraging the viewer to imagine the story.

Common subjects of street art include political messages, anti-commercialism, or spoof ads. There are different styles of graffiti lettering used, some of which interlock letters, making them harder to read.

Mark Bodé works as a cartoonist for American comic books. He has also taken up spray can art to collaborate with fellow artist "Cuba" on murals, such as this one on North Beach, in San Francisco.

Work in art

From the manic modern day **stress** shown below in *Deadline* to the sweaty and tough **rural farming** in *The Golden Fleece*, these paintings show people from different eras and cultures at work.

◀ **Chopping tobacco**, 1893, **José Ferraz de Almeida Júnior, Oil on canvas** Almeida Júnior was a Brazilian artist famous for painting countrymen and rural landscapes. His style is influenced by Realism (see page 68).

▲ **Deadline,** late 20th century, Pamela J. Crook, **Acrylic on canvas on wood** This is a very busy scene painted with lots of strong colors. It shows the hectic bustle of modern working life. By including the frame in the picture, Crook gives the painting a three-dimensional effect.

▲ **Nihonbashi on a Snowy Day,** 1840, Ando **Hiroshige, Woodblock print** Hiroshige often depicted different seasons in his work. This detailed scene shows people trying to get to work across the Nihonbashi ("Japan bridge") in Edo (now Tokyo) in the snow.

SEEING THINGS
For more about woodblock prints see page 54–55

▲ **The Fog Warning,** 1885, Winslow Homer, Oil on **canvas** The sea was Homer's favorite subject to paint, especially showing how man copes with nature. Here, a fisherman has just seen a fog coming his way. Will he get back to his ship in time?

◀ **The Floor Strippers,** 1875, **Gustave Caillebotte, Oil on canvas**
Caillebotte was part of the Impressionist group. He often painted scenes from unusual angles and preferred his subjects not to pose, as shown here.

▲ **The Golden Fleece,** 1894, Tom Roberts, Oil on **canvas** Although his work was not appreciated during his lifetime, Roberts has since been famous for helping to develop Australia's national identity by painting farmers and sheep-shearers at work.

▲ **Akbarnama,** 16th century, Abu'l Fazi, Opaque **watercolor and gold on paper** The title of this piece means Book of Akbar, which was about the life and times of Emperor Akbar. This artwork shows his people preparing for a celebration.

Artist's biography

Friedensreich **Hundertwasser**

1928: *Born in Vienna, Austria; named Friedrich Stowasser*

1936-37: *At the age of 8, attended Montessori school to develop artistic talent*

1948: *Stayed only three months at Academy of Fine Arts, Vienna*

1949: *At age 21, changed name and began traveling*

1960: *Visited Japan for the first time*

1973: *At age 45, visited New Zealand and bought a farm as a second home*

2000: *Died on board the Queen Elizabeth 2 cruise liner*

Artist's influences

Gustav Klimt— *Influenced by the richly decorated patterns and colors*

Egon Schiele— *Influenced by the twisted body shapes*

Friedensreich **Hundertwasser**

"Paradise is here, only we are destroying it. I want to show how simple it is to have paradise on Earth!"

 The 30 Day Fax Painting, *1994, 60 x 51 in (151 x 130 cm)—Mixed media*

The Austrian-born abstract artist Friedensreich Hundertwasser created his own artistic theory, called **"transautomatism."** This theory was all about the experience of the viewer, recognizing that different people see different things when looking at a picture. Your reaction to his pictures will be different than the reactions of your friends. Hundertwasser lived a **bohemian** lifestyle and loved traveling. He rarely wore a matching jacket and pants or socks of the same color.

The Ronald McDonald House, Essen, Germany, completed in 2005

Hundertwasser was passionate about nature and believed that an artist should get inspired by the irregular patterns of nature. He saw the spiral as a symbol of the natural cycle of life and death and used them all over his paintings. There are no straight lines and even all the windows on the cars and buildings are drawn with flowing shapes.

The swirls break up the rigid outline of the window.

This picture is made up of 30 letter-sized FAXes. Notice all the bold, contrasting colors that Hundertwasser has used. He also often added gold and silver leaf for a shimmering effect.

International architect

Hundertwasser was not only a painter, but also an architect and ecologist. He designed buildings around the world, which all have his very distinctive vibrant, irregular style. Often the floors are unlevel, plants grow from the roofs and walls, and sometimes the windows are different shapes and sizes. Hundertwasser's buildings have included a power plant, a church, and public restrooms.

NOW YOU TRY...

Try drawing your own picture inspired by Hundertwasser.

Draw spirals and swirly shapes—remember no straight lines—and why not add some plants growing from the roof or out of the walls. Use bold colors to make an eye-catching masterpiece.

Danielle Taylor age 9

The public restrooms in Kawakawa, New Zealand, were designed by Hundertwasser in 1999.

The Hundertwasser house, completed in 1985, is an apartment building in Vienna, Austria.

Modern *art*

The art of the 20th century often challenges our notions of art, since art styles have taken many different directions. Just like art of the past, the art can be **experimental**, can question our ideas and our understanding of the world, and is inspired by our lifestyle.

Since the 1950s...

Cadmium is a popular shade of red.

ACRYLIC Paint

In the 1950s, a new plastic-based paint called acrylic became available. It was fast-drying, allowing artists to rework their paintings, add details, and correct mistakes by painting over the top without the color underneath showing through.

Pop artists

Pop artists, such as Andy Warhol (see page 94), adapted images of **popular culture** from advertisements and famous movie stars.

Marilyn Monroe,
1967,
by Andy Warhol

Popular Culture (1950–2000)

www
www.dk.com

World Wide Web (1989–)

Culture in the 20th century changed dramatically with the popularity of movie stars and pop stars, the desire to own material possessions, and the style of comic books and other media.

In the 1970s, home computers became increasingly popular. The World Wide Web began in 1989 and artists used this to show their work to an **international** audience and to sell to a global market.

Four Knights, *1980,*
by Gilbert and George

Around the world, there are museums that display just modern art, sponsored by public corporations or private collectors. Some of the buildings are works of art themselves.

MUSEUMS of Modern Art

Photocopiers, fax machines, scanners, digital photography, and video are just some of the **technologies** that recent artists have either used in their artworks or imitated the effects of in their art.

NEW Technologies

These are just some of the many styles modern artists still experiment with...

Installations

Hélio Oiticica
Grande Núcleo, NC3, NC4, NC6 Manifestação Ambiental n.2, *1960–1963*
Installation art is the arrangement of interesting materials to fill a specific space—such as Oiticica's colored boards suspended in a room.

Conceptual art

Piero Manzoni
Artist's Breath, *1960*
The idea, or concept, of the art is more important than what the art looks like. Manzoni's concept was to let a balloon deflate to represent a passing breath.

Photography

Ansel Adams
Jeffrey Pine, Sentinel Dome, *c. 1940*
Through experimenting with the taking and developing of photographs, Adams is known for making dramatic black and white photographs that have sharpness and depth.

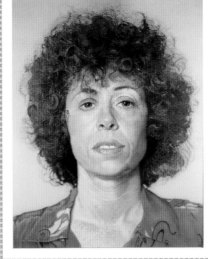

Chuck Close
Linda, *1975–1976*
Chuck Close makes paintings of photographs, by dividing each photograph into a grid, and then copying the grid onto a canvas. This type of art is known as Superrealism or Photorealism.

Performance art

Gilbert and George
Title unknown, *20th century*
The work of performance art combines theater and music. In the late 1960s, Gilbert and George featured in their work wearing their trademark suits and painted golden hands and faces as "living sculptures."

Video art

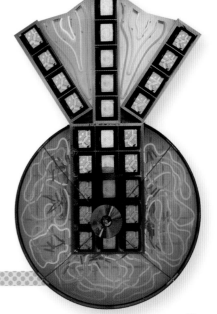

Nam June Paik
Mars, *1990*
Nam June Paik made interesting arrangements of many television screens, showing repeated recorded images of ordinary things.

Sculpture

Sculpture is the art of shaping **three-dimensional** figures or designs to be free-standing or as decoration in walls. Today, all kinds of industrial and **everyday materials** are used, as well as the traditional techniques such as stone carving or bronze casting.

Carved in stone

The story begins...

People started carving things out of stone more than **26,000 years ago**. The first sculptures were often of important people—rulers, gods, mythical creatures, or ancestors. They were often **very big**, because they were designed to impress.

Leshan Giant Buddha,
8th century
This statue of a seated Buddha is truly **enormous**—232 ft (71 m) high, with shoulders 91 ft (28 m) wide and feet 26 ft (8 m) long. It was carved out of a cliff face in Sichuan province, China. The Buddha's ears are made of wood and attached to the head.

The Willendorf Venus,
c.24,000 BCE
Some of the earliest stone sculptures made in Europe were **small figures** of naked women. This one is named after Willendorf, the Austrian village where it was found.

> Historians call me the priest-king because of my fancy clothes and jewelry, but no one knows who I really was.

Figure from Mohenjo Daro, *c.2500 BCE*
Mohenjo Daro, situated in the Indus Valley in modern-day Pakistan. The sculptures found there are among some of the **earliest** known.

The Sphinx, *c.2520–2494 BCE*
This huge figure of a mythical creature with the body of a lion and a human head guards the Pyramids at Giza in Egypt. **Egyptian figures** are generally shown looking straight ahead.

The Lion Gate at Mycenae *c.1250 BCE*
This impressive gateway is the entrance to the ancient city of Mycenae in Greece. The **two carved lionesses** (left), which originally had metal heads, are probably guarding the gateway.

Head of Nefertiti,
c.1340 BCE
Nefertiti was the wife of the pharaoh Akhenaten and was famous for her beauty. The statue consists of an inner limestone carving covered in layers of plaster, called **stucco**.

Assyrian bull figure,
713–706 BCE Standing over 13 ft (4 m) tall, this **huge mythical creature** is a lamassu—a winged bull with a human head. It is one of a pair that once stood in the palace of Sargon II, in what is now Iraq.

Olmec head, *1400–400 BCE*
The Olmec people lived in Mexico from about 1400 to 400 BCE. They produced many enormous stone sculptures of **helmeted heads**. The heads are probably Olmec rulers.

Easter Island statue,
1250–1500
This is a moai—one of hundreds of huge figures that stand on Easter Island in the Pacific. **Moai** represent the islanders' dead ancestors.

The Terra-cotta Army sculptors

In c. 246 BCE, the first emperor of China, Qin Shi Huang, commissioned over 700,000 workers to begin constructing an elaborate cemetery for him. It contained an **entire army** sculpted out of clay, which would enable Qin to rule another empire in the afterlife.

Qin Shi Huang was obsessed with finding the secret of immortality (living forever).

The discovery of the Terra-cotta Army has excited the world. It is now hailed as **the eighth wonder** of the ancient world!

In 1974, local farmers in Xian, China, were building a well when they dug into a pit by accident. The pit contained **thousands** of life-size terra-cotta warriors. Further excavation was carried out and in 1976 two more pits were discovered with even more figures.

Each warrior could be up to 6½ ft (2 m) tall and weigh around 660 lbs (300 kg). There were different types of warrior, including crossbowmen, charioteers, officers, and generals.

A grand production

It took more than 700,000 local craftsmen and laborers to complete the Terra-cotta Army for the emperor. In order to carry out a task on such a large scale, each worker had a specific part to do, just like in a factory assembly line. Amazingly, each warrior sculpture was **unique**. Height, uniform, and hairstyle varied depending on a warrior's rank within the army. Each sculpture was also **very detailed**—even the soles of their boots had tread patterns!

When they were discovered in 1974, some of the terra-cotta warriors were broken or cracked. However, most of them were able to be **restored**. Modern historians have also learned that each warrior was put together using separate parts, rather than from one piece of terra-cotta. They even found workshop names on each separate part.

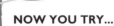

NOW YOU TRY...

Qin Shi Huang was just 13 years old when the construction of the Terra-cotta Army began!

Look at this photo of clay warrior models made by children at the British Museum, London.

Can you think of any sculptures you would like to have built for you?

Models from a children's workshop at the British Museum

109

How to carve
wood

Wood can be sculpted by using a cutting tool to shape it into a figure or decorative design. Skilled **wood carvers** around the world have used wood for everything from mask-making to house-building.

Totem pole style

Traditionally made by tribal groups of Native Americans along the northwest coast, **totem poles** are made from red cedar trees, which can grow up to 200 ft (61 m) tall and are less likely to decay than other wood. Totem poles can vary in height from 10–100 ft (3 to 30 m) and their designs are complex. They represent the **ancestral myths** specific to particular families, showing the family crest (which is often a forest or mountain animal), an ancestoral figure, and a mythical or partly historical event.

Wood carving timeline

Carving wood to make decorative features or sculpting into figures has been a tradition since ancient times.

c. 1327 BCE *This golden wooden statue of Tutankhamun riding on the back of a black leopard was found in the boy pharaoh's tomb, representing his passage into the afterlife.*

Date unknown *The wooden Tiki face carvings of the Maori people of New Zealand might represent ancestors of a tribe, but mostly are a decorative feature.*

c. 1407 *The five-story pagoda at the Itsukushima Jinja shrine in Japan has a typical style of large overhangs on the roofs.*

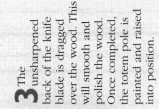

Here's how to carve a totem pole

1 Prepare the wood for carving by removing the bark, then draw the design onto the wood. For large totem poles, an elbow adze is used to cut out large chunks roughly.

2 A curved knife is used to cut out the details. Small shavings are taken away bit by bit to work up the desired shape. The tool is held with the blade coming out of the bottom of the fist, and the knife is pulled toward the carver.

3 The unsharpened back of the knife blade is dragged over the wood. This will smooth and polish the wood. Once completed, the totem pole is painted and raised into position.

1501–05 *Tilman Riemenschneider was a German sculptor who worked mainly with wood, making intricate carvings of figures. Many of his works still exist in churches in Germany, such as this one of* The Last Supper *(detail shown).*

17th century *Grinling Gibbons became well-known in his day for his decorative woodwork, such as carvings of fruits, garlands, and animals.*

1969 *Louise Nevelson became famous for her sculpted and painted wooden walls of many boxes filled with abstract shapes and familiar objects, such as* Mirror Image 1.

20th century *Stephan Balkenhol chisels his individual figures from a single block of wood. The surfaces are rough with chisel marks, which are left to create shadows, making the figure seem alive. He paints his sculptures but leaves the skin unpainted*

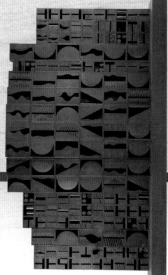

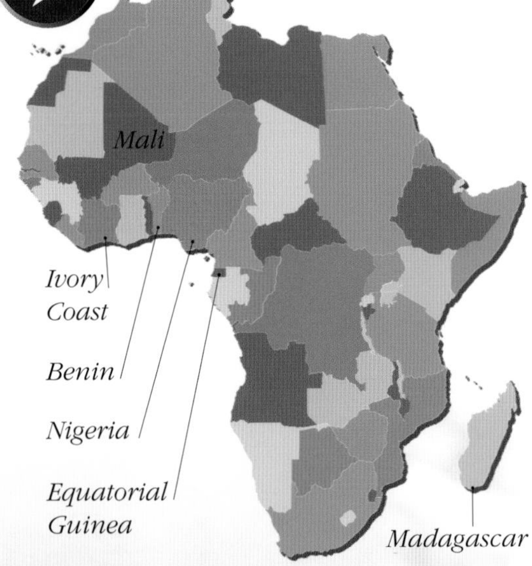

African sculpture

African sculptures are almost always inspired by the human figure, but they can be made from many different materials, including stone, animal horn, bronze, terra-cotta, and wood. Masks, heads, and figurines are produced in many parts of Africa, each with its own **regional style**. These objects are not designed to be hung on a wall or exhibited in a museum, but to be used, often in **religious ceremonies**.

Mali

Ivory Coast

Benin

Nigeria

Equatorial Guinea

Madagascar

Dogon mask
The Dogon people of Mali carve more than 80 types of wooden mask. Some masks are thought to have magical powers, while others represent animals or people.

Fang mask
This mask was made by the Fang people from Equatorial Guinea. Called a *ngil*, it features a long face and is painted with white kaolin clay.

Figure of an Oba
This bronze statue depicts an **Oba**, a ruler of the Ife kingdom, which flourished in modern-day Nigeria from about 700 to 900 CE. The statue is a bronze cast, made from a clay model of the figure.

Ibeji twin figure
The Yoruba people of Nigeria often have twins. If one twin dies, a sculptor creates a small wooden figure called an *ibeji* (twin) to represent the lost child. The mother keeps the figure and cares for it.

Madagascan grave markers
The Mahafaly people of Madagascar mark graves with carved wooden posts and zebu horns. The carvings depict **events** in the dead person's life.

Dan masks These carved wooden masks from Ivory Coast are made and worn by male dancers. Once a dancer puts on a mask, the Dan believe he is transformed into the **spirit or ancestor** that the mask represents.

Romuald Hazoumé
This Benin artist creates sculptures from **junk**, such as old cans, jugs, and video boxes. Many of his works resemble traditional African masks. This one is called *Gbakounon*.

113

Parthenon frieze (detail)
*447–432 BCE, 524 ft- (160 m-)
long—Marble*

Marble timeline

*The style of sculpting marble has developed through history,
but the skill of the sculptors has always been impressive.*

447–432 BCE *The Parthenon frieze
established the Classical Greek style
of sculpting the perfect figure.*

c. 1st century BCE–c. 5th century CE
*During Roman times, the city of
Aphrodisias in Turkey was famous
for its sculpture school.*

15th century *Renaissance artist
Donatello revived the Classical style
to create realistic statues such as
this of St. John.*

17th century *Gianlorenzo Bernini was
a skillful Baroque sculptor whose work
included busts of kings and patrons.*

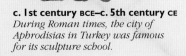

How to sculpt marble

Many sculptors have used a **crystalized limestone rock** known as marble for their sculptures. Marble is found in a great variety of colors and patterns and can be **polished** for a stunning effect.

Here's how to sculpt marble

Sculpting marble is a slow process. It requires a lot of patience, slowly chipping away with a hammer and chisel until the block of marble takes the shape of the sculpture.

1 *Holding a heavy or point chisel against the stone, the sculptor swings the hammer at the chisel as hard as possible. Then any chips are flicked out of the way, before repositioning the chisel for the next blow. In this way the shape of the sculpture is "roughed out."*

2 *A flat chisel is used to create the details and refine the sculpture. Once finished, the ancient Greeks would have used a stone called an emery to smooth the chipped surface, but today a sculptor might use wet sandpaper. Finally, the sculpture is polished for shine. The Greeks used a softer stone for this.*

The Greek sculptor Phidias designed and supervised the construction of the Parthenon in Athens, including the sculptural frieze that went around the top of the inner columns.

Sculptors would take months, if not years, to complete their works, slowly chipping away with their hammers and various chisels.

Classical Greek style

Between 480 BCE and 300 BCE, ancient Greek sculptors developed a realistic and **idealistic** style now known as Classical. They would sculpt their idea of the "perfect" human figure, giving it **natural features** and making it young and athletic. Dressing the figures in flowing robes gave the impression of **movement**. The Greek sculptor Phidias was influential in developing this style.

c.1770s *This expressive portrait bust of the Russian queen Catherine II is by Marie-Anne Collot, a pupil of the French Rococo sculptor Etienne-Maurice Falconet.*

1800–05 *Aleijadinho had leprosy, but managed to carve figures using a hammer and chisel tied to his fingerless hands.*

1886–1901 *Auguste Rodin broke new ground with his unfinished and often exaggerated style, as seen in The Storm.*

1913 *The simple style of Jacob Epstein's* Mother and Child *was inspired by prehistoric and African sculpture.*

Michelangelo Buonarroti

Michelangelo, c. 1540, by Daniele da Volterra

"However rich I may have been, I have always lived like a poor man."

Michelangelo had a career in art that spanned more than 70 years! During this time he was considered the best artist in Europe. He worked tirelessly on scaffolding for over four years painting the ceiling of the **Sistine Chapel** in Rome, Italy. Although Michelangelo is famous for this fantastic fresco, he thought of himself as a **sculptor**.

In the biblical story of David and Goliath, only David—then a young shepherd boy—was brave enough to fight the giant.

David

Michelangelo finished sculpting the biblical figure of David in 1504. The statue soon became a symbol of **strength** for the newly formed Republic of Florence. David was seen as a brave and loyal fighter for **freedom**, which was the way the citizens of Florence viewed themselves.

This is an early sketch of *David* holding his slingshot, which Michelangelo drew for inspiration. Michelangelo believed that every piece of stone had a sculpture already in it, so it was up to the sculptor to simply set free the figure within.

David is shown holding a sling in his hand, which would be would use to throw the rock that killed the giant Goliath.

Artist's biography

Michelangelo **Buonarroti**

1475: Born in Tuscany, Italy

1488: At age 13 he became an artist's apprentice, but a year later joined a sculptor's academy

1490–1492: Worked in Florence and came into contact with the powerful Medici family

1496–1501: Worked in Rome as a sculptor

1501: At age 26, started sculpting the biblical King David as a shepherd boy. The finished sculpture was unveiled in Florence three years later

1508–1512: Painted the ceiling of the Sistine Chapel in Rome

1564: Died at age 88

Artist's influences

Verrocchio's David— Inspired by the sculpting of idealized figures of male heroes

The original David was moved into the Academy Gallery in Florence in 1873. In 2003, the statue was cleaned with distilled water to remove the 500 years of dirt.

David's perfect nose

Giorgio Vasari, Michelangelo's biographer, tells an amusing story about a nobleman who thought David's nose was too large. On hearing this, Michelangelo appeared to chisel away at the nose, with bits of dust and marble falling to the floor. The nobleman exclaimed that the nose was now perfect. However, Michelangelo had in fact taken a handful of marble dust from his pocket and had only pretended to chisel!

At over 17 ft (5 m) tall, David is about three times the height of an adult person.

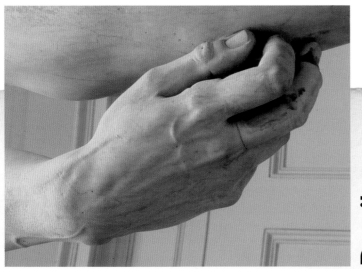

Detail
Michelangelo was very eager to show the human form in a lifelike way. Some sources say he **dissected** corpses so that he could learn how the muscular system worked. His David was as detailed and realistic as possible.

In a break with tradition, Michelangelo wanted to show David before the fight, looking deep in thought, rather than as a hero after the battle.

117

Frédéric-Auguste Bartholdi

"From her beacon-hand Glows world-wide welcome"
(from The New Colossus by Emma Lazarus)

Frédéric Auguste Bartholdi
1834–1904
Bartholdi was very patriotic and the *Lion of Belfort* was a memorial to the town of Belfort's brave defense during the Franco-German war (1870–71).

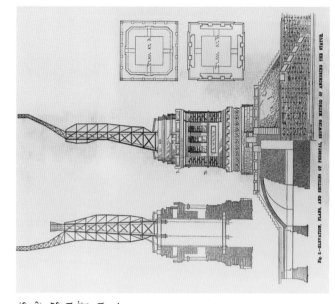

The Frenchman Bartholdi first studied painting and architecture in Paris. However, he quickly realized that sculpture was his main passion, which he focused on for the rest of his life. He became well-known for two **monumental sculptures:** the *Lion of Belfort,* carved in sandstone, and the even larger *Statue of Liberty,* made of copper sheets. This statue was a gift from the French to the United States to celebrate their friendship during the Revolutionary War (1775–1783).

The statue, also known as *Liberty Enlightening the World,* was sculpted using wooden molds, with an exterior shell of copper and an iron interior structure.

Statue of Liberty

Designed by Bartholdi, the statue was constructed by **Gustave Eiffel,** who went on to create the Eiffel Tower in Paris, France. The statue stands on Liberty Island, New York. As one of the biggest statues ever created, each year over 2 million visitors come to take a look. It has become a **symbol of freedom** worldwide.

On Liberty's crown there are seven rays, representing the seven seas and seven continents.

Sculptor's biography
Frédéric-Auguste **Bartholdi**

1834: *Born in Alsace, France*

1856: *At age 22 traveled to Egypt and was inspired by the monumental works he saw there*

1874–1886: *Construction of Statue of Liberty*

1879: *Earned US patent for Statue of Liberty*

1880: *At age 46 completed Lion of Belfort, based in eastern France*

1904: *Died in Paris*

Artist's influences

Egyptian sculpture—
Inspired by the large, sturdy, and simple qualities of Egyptian monuments

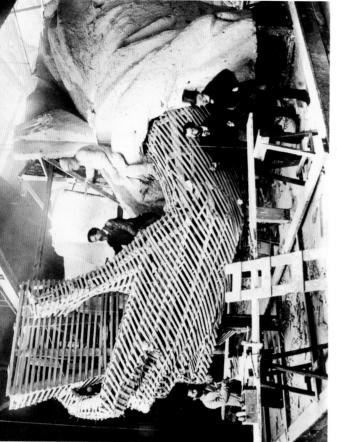

A monumental delivery

After Gustave Eiffel constructed the statue, it was dismantled for shipping across the Atlantic Ocean to New York, where it was **reassembled** and finally dedicated to the United States in 1886. It took over 214 large wooden crates to transport all the pieces!

The *Statue of Liberty's* head and shoulders were displayed at the Paris World's Fair in June 1878. **Funding** for constructing the statue was running low but luckily showing Liberty's head at the fair stirred up lots of enthusiasm. The French government decided to allow a lottery to take place in order to raise more money so Bartholdi and Eiffel could complete the statue.

Liberty holds a tablet with the date of the Declaration of Independence engraved on it—July 4, 1776.

On the base of the statue, inscribed in bronze, is a sonnet by the poet Emma Lazarus. The sonnet is called The New Colossus and was written in 1883.

Bertel Thorvaldsen —*Influenced by the realistic features of the Lion Monument (1821), a grand memorial to Swiss soldiers who died during the French Revolution*

Facts and figures

151 ft (46 m): *height from base to torch*

16 ft 5 in (5 m): *length of hand*

4 ft 6 in (1.4 m): *length of nose*

450,000 pounds (204 metric tons): *total weight*

Artist's Biography
Gustav **Vigeland**

1869: *Born on a farm in Mandal, Norway*

1888: *At age 19 determined to succeed as a professional sculptor and received support and training from Norwegian sculptor Brynjulf Bergslien*

1891–1896: *Visited other European cities, including Paris, where Auguste Rodin greatly influenced him*

1894–1896: *Held his own exhibitions in Norway and built up a strong reputation in the art world*

1898–1902: *Worked on restoring the Nidaros Cathedral, Trondheim*

1921: *At age 52 began contract with the city of Oslo—he would receive a salary and his work would belong to the city*

1924: *Moved into a new studio in Kirkeveien and spent the next 19 years creating Frogner Park*

1943: *Died in Oslo*

Artist's influences

Auguste Rodin
—Inspired by the powerful human forms and realistic style created by Rodin, as well as the intimate relationship between man and woman (**The Thinker**, *1880–82, Bronze*)

Gustav **Vigeland**

Norwegian sculptor, Gustav Vigeland, made a **unique contract** with the city of Oslo. He was to be paid a salary and given a studio to work in, and in return, all his work belonged to the city. This was when he began on his most **ambitious** project—Vigeland Sculpture Park.

A long, straight walkway runs through the middle of the park, from the Main Gate, over the Bridge, past the fountain to the Wheel of Life.

Let's go on a journey of life

The main theme of Vigeland's work is a human's journey **from cradle to grave**. These sculptures (right) show an unborn baby, children playing, then adult life and parenthood. Typically, Vigeland's sculptures show people engaged in **ordinary activities**—as well as emotions from love and happiness to anger and grief.

Vigeland Sculpture Park

In this park are more than **200** bronze and granite sculptures of nude figures. They were all designed by Gustav Vigeland, then carved and cast by his team of highly skilled assistants. The park covers **80 acres** (320,000 square meters) and is part of the larger Frogner Park. The sculpture park was mainly built between 1939 and 1949.

Wheel of Life

This bronze wheel is a garland of people holding on to each other. It represents life going on forever. Vigeland was pleased with his wheel. He said, "I have never been as accomplished as I am now."

Vigeland Park is the largest sculpture park made by a single artist.

The Bridge

Fifty-eight sculptures of men, women, and children stand along the edge of the Bridge. Here, in pairs, groups, or alone, they illustrate **human relationships** and emotions. Vast lanterns stand between them.

These statues are carved in granite.

Abstract **sculpture**

The 20th century was a period when sculptors tried out lots of new ideas and techniques. Some sculptors were inspired by steel, glass, and other industrial materials and used **industrial techniques**, such as welding. Others experimented with newly invented materials, such as plastic, or made moving sculptures. But the one thing they had in common was their **abstract style**.

Barbara Hepworth (1903–1975)

Hepworth lived in the coastal town of St. Ives in southwest England, and her work was inspired by the landscape, rocks, and sea around her.

Pierced Form (Toledo), *1957, Mahogany*

Hepworth's sculptures were often hollowed out or featured holes.

Hepworth worked in bronze, wood, and marble, and many of her pieces were made to be displayed outside.

Oval Sculpture, *1959, Bronze*

How did it happen?

Abstract sculptors were inspired by the ground-breaking work of the 19th century sculptor **Auguste Rodin,** and earlier abstract art, partieularly Cubism and the works of **Picasso** (see page 72).

Auguste Rodin
The Storm, *1886–1901,*
Rodin's rough, unfinished, or simplified figures broke with the previous tradition of representing things as realistically as possible.

Constantin Brâncuși
The Kiss, *1907-08*
In his sculptures, Brâncusi tried to reveal the essence of his subject, rather than copying its outward appearance. Brâncusi's work paved the way for later, more abstract sculptors.

David Smith

Cubi XXVIII, *1965*

The American sculptor David Smith created large, abstract steel sculptures, inspired by the welded sculptures of González and Picasso. His most famous works are his *Cubi* sculptures, made in the 1960s, which feature squares, rectangles, and other **geometric shapes**. Over the years, Smith's sculptures got bigger and bigger, and they were designed to be displayed outside.

Alexander Calder

Three Tentacles, *1975*

The American sculptor Alexander Calder is famous for inventing "**mobiles,**" named by the artist Marcel Duchamp. Calder's most recognizable mobiles are his later sculptures, which were carefully **balanced compositions** of wire and sheet metal that could move with the slightest breeze.

Barbara Hepworth

Sculpture with Strings,
1939 (cast 1961)

Hepworth's sculptures were abstract, but often depicted landscapes or human figures. She would go on vacation with other sculptors, including Henry Moore (see page 124), and share ideas.

Julio González

Cactus Man No.1, *1939–40*

González was a Spanish abstract sculptor, famous for his welded metal sculptures. He learned how to work with metal in his father's forge and while in a car factory in France, he learned **oxyacetylene welding**—a mix of fuel gases and oxygen in a welding torch.

Naum Gabo

Head of a Woman, *c. 1917–20*

Gabo was one of the first people to make **kinetic** (moving) art. He worked with industrial materials such as wood, metals, glass, and plastic and his work was important to the development of **Constructivism** in art. This sculpture, called *Head of a Woman*, is made from celluloid, one of the earliest types of plastic.

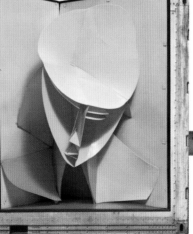

Henry **Moore**

"All art should have a certain mystery and should make demands on the spectator."

Henry Moore was born into a mining family in Yorkshire, England, as one of eight children. At age 11, he decided that he wanted to be a sculptor and went on to become the most famous British sculptor of the 20th century. His work is more inspired by **tribal and ancient art** than by the traditional ideas of beauty shown in Renaissance sculptures and paintings.

Recurring reclining figures

Many of Moore's sculptures are of the female form in a reclining position. The smooth **curves** of these sculptures have been linked to the rolling landscape of Moore's hometown in Yorkshire. Another common theme in Moore's work is that of **mother and child**. This became an important part of his work after his first child, Mary, was born.

This piece is called *Large Reclining Figure* and was displayed at Kew Gardens, London. Moore used **fiberglass** for this sculpture as it is a lightweight material and can be moved more easily than bronze.

Later on in Moore's career, **bronze** rather than stone became his favorite method for creating large-scale sculptures.

Reclining figure: Right Angles, *1981—Bronze*

Artist's biography
Alberto **Giacometti**

1901: *Born in Borgonovo, Switzerland, the son of painter Giovanni Giacometti*

1922: *At age 21 moved to Paris to be an apprentice of Émile-Antoine Bourdelle, a sculptor who worked for Auguste Rodin*

1927-1935: *Worked in a Surrealist style*

1941-1944: *During WWII, stayed in Switzerland before returning to Paris*

1947: *Created* Man Pointing *overnight for his first exhibition*

1962: *At age 61, won the acclaimed sculpture prize with a show of over 100 works at the Venice Biennale*

1966: *Died of heart disease*

Artist's influences

Max Ernst
—Inspired by the new methods being used by artists and sculptors in the Dada and Surrealism style (see page 78)

Alberto **Giacometti**

"I am not sculpting the human figure, but rather 'the shadow that is cast.'"

Large Woman II, one of a series of four figures.

A Swiss sculptor and painter who worked in Paris during the 20th century, Giacometti is best known for his **very tall**, **very thin, figures**. Early in his career, he was inspired by African and Oceanic art, and by Cubism and Surrealism. Later, he began working from nature, and for a time he was obsessed with creating **miniscule sculptures**. Eventually, he moved into the distinctive style we associate with his name.

Before his first New York exhibition, Giacometti worked with Man Pointing (left) *all night. When it was collected the next day, the plaster was still wet.*

Seeking perfection

Giacometti was a perfectionist who often **remade** his figures again and again. Even when he became enormously famous and successful, he still **destroyed** work he didn't like, or put it aside to take up again years later.

Fragile masterpiece
One of Giacometti's best-known pieces, *Man Pointing* (1947) is made of bronze and stands 5¾ x 3 ft (1.75 m x 90 cm) tall.

Most of Giacometti's females are still, while his males are active in some way. This piece is called Walking Man (1960).

The artist's view

Like all Giacometti's figures, *Walking Man* (1947) (left) has arms, legs, and a body that are much longer, thinner, and more **fragile** than a real person. Many experts believe that these frail, lonely, tense figures reveal the artist's **sad** view of the world.

NOW YOU TRY:

Play with Giacometti-like figures by forming skinny people or animals out of pipe cleaners or other flexible wire. Try making some that are standing still and some that are reaching or bending.

Kelly Foot, age 7

This sculpted head (called a bust) is the artist's friend Elie Lotar. Giacometti didn't want his busts to look like their subject, but he did want them to express each subject's personality.

How is a bronze sculpture made?

To make a bronze figure, the "lost wax" method was used to make Giacometti's sculptures (this is Giacometti, right). Today, this method starts by hand-making a **clay model** with all the detail and texture that will appear on the bronze. When the clay dries, it is covered with several coats of plaster or a liquid rubber mixture that picks up every bit of this detail.

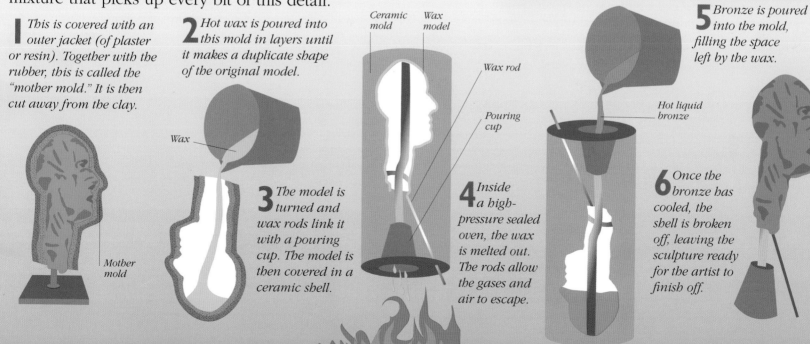

1 *This is covered with an outer jacket (of plaster or resin). Together with the rubber, this is called the "mother mold." It is then cut away from the clay.*

Wax

Mother mold

2 *Hot wax is poured into this mold in layers until it makes a duplicate shape of the original model.*

3 *The model is turned and wax rods link it with a pouring cup. The model is then covered in a ceramic shell.*

Ceramic mold   Wax model

Wax rod

Pouring cup

4 *Inside a high-pressure sealed oven, the wax is melted out. The rods allow the gases and air to escape.*

5 *Bronze is poured into the mold, filling the space left by the wax.*

Hot liquid bronze

6 *Once the bronze has cooled, the shell is broken off, leaving the sculpture ready for the artist to finish off.*

How to create Land art

Land artists use materials such as stone, branches, and leaves to create their works, and often place them in a **natural setting**. In the late 1960s this form of art became very popular, and an avid interest was taken in prehistoric earthworks. Some artworks are in **remote places** and others can only be seen from an aircraft.

Goldsworthy's style

The British Land artist Andy Goldsworthy creates his work in many different natural settings. The materials he has used include leaves, pebbles, twigs, sand, and even snow and ice. Many of his works don't exist for very long, crumbling down or melting away. Goldsworthy considers this to be the final stage of the work.

"Each work grows, stays, decays..."

Sentinel at Asse Valley, French Alps, *2000*

Land art timeline

The mystery continues about just how prehistoric and ancient people created their ground markings and boulder monuments. Their purpose was linked with rituals rather than purely artistic.

c. 3000–1600 BCE *The huge slabs that form the English stone circle of Stonehenge were hauled hundreds of miles from Wales.*

c. 2560 BCE *Thousands of workers toiled for decades to quarry and prepare the stones used to build the pyramids in Giza, Egypt.*

c. 200 BCE–700 CE *There are hundreds of large-scale ground markings in the Nazca Desert in Peru that are only visible from the air.*

Andy Goldsworthy experiments with shapes and materials before constructing his artworks in open ground.

How "on earth" does he do it?

Goldsworthy's art follows a natural cycle of construction and destruction:

• He uses **natural materials** from the site location. The only tools used are natural objects also found at the site.

• The materials are given the shape of something else **found** in nature, such as leaves placed into a spiral like a snail shell, or rocks formed into an egg.

• A **color photograph** is taken to record the work, and the work is then left to the elements.

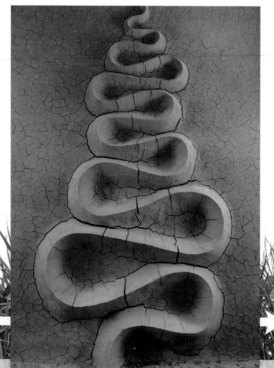

1970 Spiral Jetty *is an earthwork by Robert Smithson. Made from basalt rocks and earth, the coil is 1,500 ft (460 m) long.*

1983 *Goldsworthy's* Sand Wiggle *makes the most of the natural materials of the site to capture the effects of early morning sunlight.*

1995 *Christo and Jeanne-Claude have become famous for wrapping landmarks in materials. Their work has included the German parliament building, the Reichstag, in Berlin.*

Sculpture NOW

Sculptors today use new and even **unusual materials** such as steel, textiles, chrome, and recycled objects. There are many **huge sculptures** on display outside for the public to see and some are sited in strange places, such as on rooftops or beaches.

Jeff Koons
Balloon Dog (Yellow), *1994–2000*
Like many sculptors, Koons doesn't make his sculptures, but he does come up with the ideas for them. He is known for depicting familiar, everyday objects often in humorous ways. This oversized, smooth, and shiny balloon dog, made from reflective stainless steel, is part of his Celebration series about familiar things in childhood.

Anthony Gormley
Angel of the North, *1994–1998*
Many of Gormley's works are based on molds taken from his body. He also chooses effective locations for his works. The *Angel of the North* in Gateshead, UK, is said to be one of the most-viewed pieces of art in the world.

The sculpture is 150 ft (46 m) tall and stands at the south entrance to Chihuahua city.

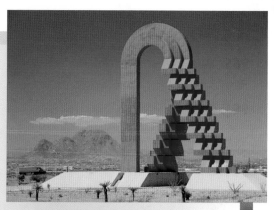

Sebastian
La Puerta de Chihuahua, *1992*
La Puerta de Chihuahua means "The Door to Chihuahua," Sebastian's home state in Mexico. Sebastian uses steel, aluminum, and cardboard to make his sculptures, creating striking geometric shapes that symbolize the balance between object and space.

Donald Judd
Untitled, *c. 1970s*
Judd believed that art should not represent anything. It should stand on its own and simply exist. Many of his works used simple, often repeated cubes or boxes to explore space and the use of space. He thinks of his sculptures as "objects" made using industrial processes.

Donald Judd's sculptures are examples of the idea of Minimal art.

Magdalena Abakanowicz
Hurma (Crowd), *1994–95*
From Poland, Abakanowicz is famous for making human bodies, or parts of them, from many different materials. At different periods, she has used rope, sackcloth, and metals. This group of 250 child and adult life-size headless figures represents the helplessness of the human condition.

Anish Kapoor
Cloud Gate, *1999-2005*
Kapoor makes enormous metal sculptures with simple, curved shapes. Some are brightly colored, while others have mirror surfaces, which make the reflected surroundings part of the work, such as this sculpture in Chicago. In this sculpture, the viewers also become part of the art, since their reflection can be seen.

Cloud Gate is 33 ft (10 m) high and it is so-called because 80 percent of the reflection is the sky.

Sculptor's biography
Damien **Hirst**

1965: *Born in Bristol, England, UK*

1986: *At age 21, studied fine art at Goldsmiths, University of London, for three years*

1988: *Organized* Freeze *exhibition of students' art in a disused building in London's docklands area*

1991: *At age 26, created* The Physical Impossibility of Death in the Mind of Someone Living—*a shark in formaldehyde that made him famous (or infamous), and has his first solo exhibition in London*

1991-2003: *Work funded by millionaire art collector Charles Saatchi*

1995: *At age 30, won the Turner Prize for* Mother and Child, Divided *(1993)—a cow and calf sliced in half*

1998: *Published autobiography*

2007: *Created* For the Love of God

2008: *Held a two-day auction of his work, called* Beautiful Inside my Head, *selling directly to the public. The sale raised $167 million*

Sculptor's inspiration
Hirst was inspired by the nightmarish work of the Irish artist Francis Bacon. Bacon shows twisted figures with grotesque, smudged features.

Self Portrait, *1969 by Francis Bacon*

Is this the most expensive piece of contemporary art? Price tag: $75 million.

The pear-shaped pink diamond in the forehead weighs 52.40 carats and worth $6 million.

The work cost $21 million to produce and was put on sale in 2007 with an asking price of $75 million. This would be the highest price ever paid for a work by a living artist. But Hirst has never revealed if the work has been sold.

For his molar Hirst used a human skull thought to have belonged to a 35-year-old person who lived between 1720 and 1810.

For the Love of God, *2007, Life-size human skull—Platinum, diamonds, and human teeth*

Damien Hirst

"For the love of God, what are you going to do next?" (Damien Hirst's mother—This question, directed at Hirst, is said to have inspired the title of the work opposite)

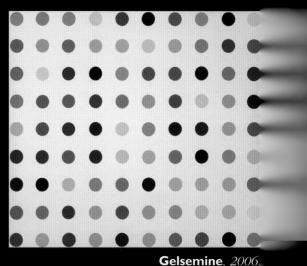

Hirst is a sculptor, **installation artist**, painter, and printmaker. He is both famous and controversial: his works sell for enormous prices, and they provoke **debates** about what is considered art. Is this art? You decide!

The Physical Impossibility of Death in the Mind of Someone Living, *1991, Glass, steel, silicon, formaldehyde solution, and shark*

Obsession with death

Death is a central theme in Hirst's works. *For the Love of God* is a platinum cast of a real skull encrusted with 8,601 diamonds. It is a kind of **memento mori**—an object intended to remind us of death. This combines two ideas that Hirst is known for: death and the value of his work. He first became famous for a series of works in which **dead animals** (including a tiger shark, a sheep, and a cow) are preserved—sometimes having been dissected—in glass cases filled with a solution containing a toxic, colorless gas called formaldehyde.

Sparkling skulls

Hirst said that the idea for his work *For the Love of God* came from seeing an Aztec skull at the British Museum, London. The Aztecs—the ruling empire in central Mexico in the 15th and 16th centuries—made wooden masks covered in **turquoise** to represent their gods.

Gelsemine, *2006 Household gloss on canvas*

Spots

Aside from his three-dimensional work, Hirst has also created lots of paintings of spots, such as this piece. The **spot paintings** are made by a random process and not directly by Hirst himself. They can be instantly identified as his work though.

Get up close to the real thing!

Many of the paintings and sculptures found in this book are exhibited in art museums and galleries. So why not plan a visit to see them for yourself?

Many countries have national or city museums or museums of modern art and these are always worth a visit. But keep your eyes open for local art galleries exhibiting works by local artists, or interesting sculpture in a nearby park, or a café selling works of art.

No one knows who the next big name in art will be. It could be the person who tries out a new style and leads art in a new direction. Maybe one day it could be you!

Cold Dark Matter: An Exploded View, *1991, by Cornelia Parker—Pieces of an exploded shed and its contents*

Glossary

Abstract an art style of the 20th century where subjects are unrecognizable and shapes and colors represent artists' emotions.

Academy a school in which art is taught, or a group of artists who are experts in a particular style of painting.

Acrylic paint a plastic-based, fast-drying paint invented in the 1950s.

Action painting a style of abstract art where the "act" of painting becomes the subject.

Apprentice a young person being taught the art of drawing, painting, and preparing materials by a master painter.

Architect a person who designs buildings and prepares exact drawings for a builder to follow.

Art Nouveau an art style beginning in the 1890s inspired by floral and stylized curvy motifs.

Automatism the technique of producing Surrealist art in a random and uncontrolled way accessing the unconscious mind.

Avant-garde a style of art that is starting a new trend or direction and is innovative or experimental.

Baroque a style of art and architecture in Europe in the 17th century that was grand and dramatic.

Biomorphism the painting of non-geometric shapes to suggest living things.

Binder an ingredient in paint that makes the pigment particles stick to each other and the paper or canvas.

Blaue Reiter, Der a group of Expressionist artists, founded in 1911 in Germany by Vassily Kandinsky and Franz Marc. The name means "Blue Rider," because they liked blue and horses.

Book of Hours an illustrated medieval religious book of prayers.

Bronze a metal alloy of copper and tin used for making statues. It also refers to a coppery-brown color.

Byzantine art the art of the eastern part of the Roman Empire between 330 and 1453. It was based on religious Christian themes and includes mosaics and icons.

Calligraphy the art of lettering in a decorative or ornamental style using a brush or pen.

Charcoal burnt wood used for drawing.

Chiaroscuro the creation of a strong contrast of light and shade in painting to suggest depth and drama.

Classical art the art of the ancient Greeks and Romans. The style showed lifelike and detailed poses and expressions. It is still used to describe things that have a perfect form.

Collage a picture or design that uses different materials stuck to a flat surface to give it an interesting texture or three-dimensional appearance.

Composition the placing or arranging of elements in an artwork to give a pleasing or particular effect.

Conceptual art an art style where the idea or concept of the art is more important than what the art looks like.

Constructivism a style of abstract modern art developed in Russia after the Revolution in 1917 to reflect the country's new industrial society.

Cubism an art style beginning in the early 1900s that painted subjects in a fragmented manner, as if viewed from different angles. It was started by Pablo Picasso and Georges Braque.

Dada an early 20th century art movement that ridiculed traditional art forms and contemporary culture by producing objects in unconventional forms using unconventional methods, often designed to shock.

Diptych a picture made of two panels hinged together, typically as a religious altarpiece.

Engraving a method of cutting a design into a material, usually metal or wood using a sharp tool. The surface is then inked and pressed onto paper.

Etching a process where a needle is used to scratch a design into wax applied over a metal plate. The plate is then dipped in acid, which creates grooves in the scratched areas. The wax is then removed and ink is run over the plate to collect in the grooves. The rest of the plate is then wiped clean before paper is pressed onto it.

Exhibition a public showing of a piece or collection of artwork.

Expressionism an art style beginning at the end of the 1800s that twisted and distorted the subject of the paintings to express an artist's inner emotions.

Fauvism an art style at the beginning of the 20th century with bold brushstrokes and vivid colors. The Fauves, meaning "wild beasts," were a group of artists painting in this style.

Fresco the art of painting onto wet plaster on walls.

Futurism an art style of the early 20th century celebrating technology and new inventions.

Glaze a thin, transparent coating brushed over a painting to protect it or add coloring to part of the picture.

Gold leaf very thin sheets of pure gold.

Gothic a western European style of architecture, painting, and sculpture that flourished between the 12th and 15th centuries.

Gouache a heavy, opaque watercolor paint.

Graffiti a drawing or inscription on a wall made with spray paint.

Hieroglyphics an ancient Egyptian form of writing that used symbols and pictures.

Illuminated manuscript a book or paper that has been decorated with richly colored drawings and occasionally silver or gold.

Impasto paint that has been put on thickly.

Impressionism term invented in 1874 to describe a style of painting originating in France in the 1860s. Impressionist painters often painted outdoors, where they were interested in the effects of light and color, and used rapid brushstrokes to gain an "impression" of the subjects of their paintings.

Installation art an arrangement of interesting materials to fill a specific space.

Land art an art style where artists use natural materials and often site their work in a natural setting.

Landscape a painting of scenery, such as mountains, rivers, trees, and fields.

Mannerism an art style that developed between 1520 and 1600.

Mosaic the art of creating images with small pieces of colored glass, stone, pottery, or other hard material.

Mural a large painting made on a wall.

Naïve art the work of artists with little or no formal art training.

Neo-Impressionism an art style beginning in the 1880s also known as Pointillism that experimented with using small dots to build up a painting.

Oil paint slow-drying paint made by mixing pigments with an oil.

Pastels a stick of color made from powdered pigment mixed with a binder, such as a resin or gum.

Performance art an art style where artists combine their art with theater and music.

Perspective the representation of three-dimensional space on a two-dimensional surface.

Petroglyph an image drawn on a rock, as in prehistoric or Aboriginal art.

Photographic art an art style where artists experiment with the taking and developing of photographs.

Pigment a powdered color that is mixed with a binder, such as gum, oil, or acrylic to make paints, pastels, or chalks.

Pop art an art style beginning in the mid-1900s that was inspired by and mimicked popular culture.

Portraits the painting of people either as head and shoulders or full-length. Self portraits are paintings by the artists of themselves.

Postimpressionism the term used to describe an art style that followed Impressionism, responding to the style, taking it further, and sometimes challenging its ideals.

Realism an art style beginning in the 1850s showing life in a realistic way, often depicting everyday subjects.

Regionalism an American art style that shows simple idyllic country life.

Renaissance the style of art and architecture in Europe in the 15th and 16th centuries. The name means "rebirth" and describes the renewed interest in Classical art.

Rococo an elegant and light-hearted style of art and architecture popular in Europe during the 18th century.

Romanticism a 19th century movement where some artists painted in a bold, dramatic, or emotional style.

Sfumato meaning smoky, a technique where sharp outlines are blurred and effects of light and shadow are created.

Silkscreen a stenciling process where sections of an illustration are blocked out of a screen of silk or mesh so that when ink is applied, areas are left blank. Further colors are then applied on top to build up a picture.

Still life a painting of objects such as fruit, furniture, and flowers.

Stucco a fine white plaster used for modeling and molding.

Superrealism an art style where paintings are made to look like photographs (also called Photorealism).

Surrealism an art style beginning around the 1920s that expressed thoughts of the unconscious mind through startling and confusing dreamlike paintings. Surreal means "more than real."

Symbolism an art style beginning in the late 1800s that explored fantasy worlds and mystery.

Tempera a type of paint in which pigment is mixed with egg yolk. It was used before the invention of oil paint.

Terra-cotta a type of reddish-brown clay.

Tesserae small tiles used to make mosaics.

Texture the surface quality or "feel" of an artwork.

Transautomatism an art style developed by Friedensreich Hundertwasser that considers the viewer's experiences toward the art.

Vanitas still-life paintings popular in the Netherlands during the 17th century, which often include symbols of death.

Video art a form of visual art that uses moving images. Unlike movies or television, it is not necessarily intended as entertainment.

Vignette an illustration without a proper border that fades into the background at its edges.

Wash a thin, transparent layer of pigment, used to cover large areas of background in watercolor painting.

Watercolors water-based paints with a transparent color quality. Paintings created with these paints are also called watercolors.

Western art the art of the European countries, and those countries that share cultural traditions with Europe—such as the nations of North America.

Woodblock prints a print made by carving designs into a block of wood. Ink is applied to the raised surfaces of the wood and transferred to paper.

Index

Acknowledgments

Dorling Kindersley would like to thank the photographers Will Heap and Jacqui Hurst, the models Catherine Greenwood (38, 52), Gertraud Goodwin (115), Martin Cheek (22), Peter Murphy (28), and Madeleine Allison (19), and the designers Karen Hood, Poppy Joslin, and Sadie Thomas.

The publisher would like to thank the following for their kind permission to reproduce their photographs: (Key: a-above; b-below/bottom; c-center; f-far; l-left; r-right; t-top)

Front Endpapers: **Alamy Images:** Robert Harding Picture Library Ltd l (Cave painting); Mary Evans Picture Library tr (Book of the dead); **The Art Archive:** Tate Gallery London/ Eileen Tweedy. © The Estate of Roy Lichtenstein/DACS 29 ca (Lichtenstein); **The Bridgeman Art Library:** Antioch, Turkey (Mosaic); British Museum c (Turner); Brooklyn Museum of Art, New York, USA/Gift of the Asian Art Council b (Thangpa); Christie's Images c (Chinese painting); Graphische Sammlung Albertina, Vienna, Austria r (Durer); National Gallery, London, UK bl (Gainsborough), tr (Lorrain); The Detroit Institute of Arts, USA/Gift of Dr. Ernest Stillman (Cassatt); Wieskirche, Wies, Germany t (Zimmermann); **Corbis:** Bettmann bl (Van Gogh); Richard Broadwell/ Beateworks cr (Rock painting); Araldo de Luca b (Roman painting); Free Agents Limited r (Maori carving); The Gallery Collection cl (Sisley), l (Van der Weyden), t (Archimboldo); Hugh Sitton/zefa tl (African masks); Gideon Mendel c (Grave marker); Rudy Sulgan tl (Pagoda); Sandro Vannini br (Masaccio); **Getty Images:** Ignacio Auzike l (Auzike); Bridgeman Art Library tl (Boccioni); Photographer's Choice tl (Terracotta army); **Brian McMorrow:** bl (mosaic); **© Tate, London 2009:** r (Sargent); Copyright the artist ca (Rego).

4 The Bridgeman Art Library: © Fernando Botero, courtesy Marlborough Gallery, New York. **6 The Bridgeman Art Library:** Private Collection) Lefevre Fine Art Ltd., London (c). **7 The Art Archive:** Tate Gallery London / Eileen Tweedy. © The Estate of Roy Lichtenstein/DACS 2009 (c). **Corbis:** Art on File/Stainless steel, 33 ft x 66 ft x 42 ft, Millennium Park, Chicago/Courtesy of the City of Chicago and Gladstone Gallery (b). **Getty Images:** Bridgeman Art Library (t). **8 iStockphoto.com:** (cr) (br). **10-11 Getty Images:** Bridgeman Art Library. **12 Alamy Images:** Robert Harding Picture Library Ltd (c); Chris Howes/Wild Places Photography (tl); Martin Jenkinson (b). **13 Clair Carnegie/ Libyan Soup:** (cl). **Joe Carnegie/Libyan Soup:** (tl) (tr). **Corbis:** Richard Broadwell/Beateworks (b). **14 Alamy Images:** Mary Evans Picture Library (b); Photofrenetic (ca) (cl). **Science Photo Library:** Michael Donne (tl) (c). **15 Corbis:** The Gallery Collection. **16 Louise Bourgeois Studio:** © DACS, London/VAGA, New York 2009. Tapestry and aluminium 14' x 12 x 12". P 35.5 x 30.4 x 30.4 cm. Private collection, courtesy Xavier Hufkens Gallery, Brussels Photo: Christopher Burke (cb). **The Bridgeman Art Library:** Collection of the Prince of Liechtenstein, Schloss Vaduz (tr). **Corbis:** Francis G. Mayer (cl); The Gallery Collection (br). **17 The Trustees of the British Museum:** (cb). **Corbis:** Christie's Images. © DACS 2009 (tr); The Gallery Collection (tl). **Finnish National Gallery:** © DACS 2009 (bl). **Fundacion Guayasamin Centro Cultural:** (br). **18 Corbis:** Alinari Archives (br); Araldo de Luca (bc) (r). **Getty Images:** Bridgeman Art Library (bl). **madderstudio.com:** (cla). 19 The Bridgeman Art Library: Detroit Industry, north wall, 1933, detail. The Detroit Institute of Arts, USA. © 2009, Banco de Mexico Diego Rivera & Frida Kahlo Museums Trust, Mexico D.F. / DACS (br); Vatican Museums and Galleries, Vatican City, Italy (bl); Nationalmuseum, Stockholm, Sweden (bc/Larsson). **Corbis:** Araldo de Luca (bc/Pozzo); Mimmo Jodice (tr). **madderstudio.com:** (cra) (cb) (crb) (tc). **20 Alamy Images:** imagebroker (cr); Ken Welsh (t). **Corbis:** Pam Gardner; Frank Lane Picture Agency (l); Penny Tweedie (br). **21 The Bridgeman Art Library:** Aboriginal Arts Agency Ltd (r) (br); Kaapa Tjampitjinpa, Goanna Dreaming (detail) Aboriginal Arts Agency Ltd (bc). **Corbis:** Hannah Mason (c); Penny Tweedie. Aboriginal Arts Agency Ltd (bl); John Van Hasselt/ Sygma (tc); Werner Forman (tl). **22 Alamy Images:** The London Art Archive (tr). **Corbis:** Ludovic Maisant (fbl). **Getty Images:** De Agostini (fbr); Medioimages / Photodisc (br). **Brian McMorrow:** (bl). **23 Courtesy Anita Shapolsky Gallery, NY:** Estate of Jeanne Reynal (br). **Emma Biggs:** photo: Tom Dunn (fbr). **Corbis:** Marco Simoni/Robert Harding World Imagery (fbl). **Julian Fong:** (tr). **Getty Images:** Gavin Hellier/Robert Harding World Imagery (tl); Keystone. © 2009, Banco de Mexico Diego Rivera & Frida Kahlo Museums Trust, Mexico D.F./DACS (bl). **Bianca Nogrady, www.biancanogrady.com:** (c). **Danielle Warner:** (cr). **24 Alamy Images:** Phil Robinson/PjrFoto/ (br). **The Bridgeman Art Library:** Louvre, Paris, France/Lauros/ Giraudon (l). **Corbis:** The Gallery Collection (tr). **Courtesy Kinsman Robinson Galleries, Toronto:** © 2008 Gabe Vadas (c). **25 The Bridgeman Art Library:** Antioch, Turkey (tr); Brooklyn Museum of Art, New York, USA/Gift of the Asian Art Council (tl); Musee Guimet, Paris, France/Bonora (br); National Gallery, London, UK (bl). **26 The Bridgeman Art Library:** People's Republic of China/Lauros / Giraudon (cr). **Corbis:** Asian Art & Archaeology, Inc. (br). **V&A Images, Victoria and Albert Museum:** (l) (cra). **27 akg-images:** Nanjing, Academy of Fine Arts, photo Gilles Mermet (tc). **The Bridgeman Art Library:** Christie's Images (tl) (cl). **Corbis:** Artkey (tr); Burstein Collection (bl); © 2008. Image copyright The Metropolitan Museum of Art/Art Resource (br). **Photo Scala, Florence:** © 2007. Image copyright The Metropolitan Museum of Art/Art Resource (cr). **28 The Bridgeman Art Library:** Musee Conde, Chantilly, France/ Giraudon (r) (ca) (cb). **29 Alamy Images:** Leslie Garland Picture Library (cra). **The Bridgeman Art Library:** Musee Conde, Chantilly, France/Giraudon (tl) (bl) (ca) (cb). **Corbis:** Sion Touhig/Sygma (tr). **30 The Bridgeman Art Library:** Musee Conde, Chantilly, France/Giraudon (cb). **Corbis:** Araldo de Luca (ca) (ftr); Sandro Vannini (bl). **DK Images:** James McConnachie (c) Rough Guides (cr); Nick Nicholls © The British Museum (tr). **Bianca Nogrady, www. biancanogrady.com:** (cl). **31 Alamy Images:** The London Art Archive (cr). **The Bridgeman Art Library:** Musee d'Unterlinden, Colmar, France (bc); National Gallery, London, UK (br). **Corbis:** Francis G. Mayer (tl) (cl); The Gallery Collection (c); Ted Spiegel (tc). **DK Images:** John Heseltine (tr). **Getty Images:** Bridgeman Art Library (bl). **32 The Bridgeman Art Library:** Private Collection (bl). **Corbis:** Burstein Collection (br); The Gallery Collection (tl). **East News Poland:** Laski Diffusion (tr). **Getty Images:** Bridgeman Art Library (cb). **33 The Bridgeman Art Library:** National Gallery, London, UK (tr); Private Collection (bl). **Corbis:** Albright-Knox Art Gallery. © ADAGP, Paris and DACS, London 2009 (tl). **McMichael Art Collection:** Gift of Margaret Thomson Tweedale, McMichael Canadian Art Collection, 1974.9.5 (cl). **Photo Scala, Florence:** © Munch Museum/Munch - Ellingsen Group, BONO, Oslo/DACS, London 2009 (br). **34 Corbis:** Gianni Dagli Orti (c). **Getty Images:** Hulton Archive (bl). **35 Corbis:** Bettmann (tl) (tr); Gianni Dagli Orti (bl) (cb). **DK Images:** Peter Chadwick (c). **Getty Images:** Bridgeman Art Library (br). **36 Corbis:** The Barnes Foundation, Merion Station Pennsylvania (bl). **Getty Images:** Bridgeman Art Library (c) (bc). **Photo Scala, Florence:** The National Gallery, London (tl). **37 Photo Scala, Florence:** The National Gallery, London (l) (br) (cr) (crb) (tr). **38 The Bridgeman Art Library:** The Iveagh Bequest, Kenwood House, London, UK (fbl); Private Collection / Christie's Images (fbr). **Corbis:** The Gallery Collection (bl) (br). **39 The Bridgeman Art Library:** The Iveagh Bequest, Kenwood House, London, UK (tr) (crb) (tl). **Corbis:** Geoffrey Clements/© ADAGP, Paris and DACS, London 2009 (bc). **Romulo Fialdini:** (bl). **© Yannis Tsarouchis Foundation:** Yannis Tsarouchis, The Four Seasons, 1969. Oil on canvas, 156.5 x 295 cm. Private Collection (br). **40 akg-images:** Kunsthistorisches Museum (c). **The Bridgeman Art Library:** Museum Narodowe, Poznan, Poland (tr); Phillips, The International Fine Art Auctioneers (cl); Prado, Madrid, Spain/ Giraudon (bl); Private Collection/© Henry Moore Foundation (br). **41 The Bridgeman Art Library:** © Fernando Botero, courtesy Marlborough Gallery, New York (tl); Nationalmuseum, Stockholm, Sweden (tr); Private Collection/ Photo 9c) Lefevre Fine Art Ltd., London (br). **Photo Scala, Florence:** Mr. and Mrs. William B. Jaffe Fund.327.1955. © 2009 Digital image, The Museum of Modern Art, New York/© Karel Appel Foundation, Amsterdam (c). **Lasar Segall, 1891 Vilna - 1957 São Paulo, Collection of the Lasar Segall Museum, São Paulo, National Institute of the Historical Artistic Patrimony, Brazilian Ministry of Culture:** (bl). **42 The Bridgeman Art Library:** Vatican Museums and Galleries, Vatican City, Italy (tc); Museo Regionale, Messina, Sicily, Italy (tr); Private Collection/Photo © Rafael Valls Gallery, London, UK (br); Schlossmuseum, Schloss Friedenstein, Gotha, Germany/Bildarchiv Foto Marburg (cl). **Corbis:** Alinari Archives (ca); Geoffrey Clements (cr); Hugh Rooney; Eye Ubiquitous (bl). **42-43 Corbis:** Arcaid (columns). **43 The Bridgeman Art Library:** Burghley House Collection, Lincolnshire, UK (c); Fitzwilliam Museum, University of Cambridge, UK (tl); Vatican Museums and Galleries, Vatican City, Italy (tr); Johnny van Haeften Gallery, London, UK (cl); Musee des Beaux-Arts, Pau, France/ Giraudon (bc); Museum of Fine Arts, Budapest, Hungary (cr); National Gallery, London, UK (br); Prado, Madrid, Spain/ Giraudon/ (tc); Private Collection/Christie's Images (bl). **44 The Bridgeman Art Library:** Rijksmuseum, Amsterdam, The Netherlands (t). **Corbis:** Burstein Collection (bc); Christie's Images (clb); Francis G. Mayer (cl) (bl) (br) (cr). **45 Corbis:** Francis G. Mayer. **46 The Bridgeman Art Library:** Musee des Beaux-Arts, Marseille, France/Giraudon (tr); Museo Archeologico Nazionale, Naples, Italy (bl). **Corbis:** Bettmann (cl); The Gallery Collection (br). **47 Corbis:** Burstein Collection (tr); Christie's Images/© DACS 2009 (tl); Francis G. Mayer. © ADAGP, Paris and DACS, London 2009 (bl). **Oya - Bülent Eczacıbaı Collection:** Chianti Bottle and Fish, Fikret Muallâ, 1903 - 1967, gouache on paper, without frame: 33 x 50 cm (br). **48 The Bridgeman Art Library:** Louvre, Paris, France (cr). **Corbis:** Christie's Images (br); Klaus Hackenberg/ zefa (tl). **Getty Images:** Manuel Cohen (bl); Digital Vision (cra); Dorling Kindersley (tr); Stone (tc). **49 The Bridgeman Art Library:** Aldo Crespi Collection, Milan, Italy (ca); Musee Lambinet, Versailles, France / Lauros / Giraudon (tr); National Gallery, London, UK (bl) (br); Stiftsmuseum, Klosterneuburg, Austria (clb); Wieskirche, Wies, Germany (cb). **Corbis:** Alinari Archives (cr); The Gallery Collection (tl). **50 The Bridgeman Art Library:** Prado, Madrid (br); Dagli Orti (bl). **Corbis:** Burstein Collection (bc); The Gallery Collection (tl). **50-51 The Bridgeman Art Library:** Prado, Madrid (c). **51 The Bridgeman Art Library:** Prado, Madrid (br). **52 Alamy Images:** Peter Barritt (cl). **The Bridgeman Art Library:** British Museum (bc); Graphische Sammlung Albertina, Vienna, Austria (bl). **The Trustees of the British Museum:** (br). **53 The Bridgeman Art Library:** British Museum (t); Brooklyn Museum of Art, New York, USA/Purchased by special subscription (fbl); Galerie Daniel Malingue, Paris/© ADAGP, Paris and DACS, London 2009 (fbr); Private Collection / © Chris Beetles, London, U.K. (bl). **Corbis:** Artkey (br). **54 Corbis:** Burstein Collection (t). **Derrel Blain,** http://www. flickr.com/people/dailyartmasomenos/ (b) **55 Corbis:** Burstein Collection (clb); Christie's Images (tc); Historical Picture Archive (fbr). **Photolibrary:** (br). **56-57 The Art Archive:** Tate Gallery London/ Eileen Tweedy. © The Estate of Roy Lichtenstein/DACS 2009. **58 The Bridgeman Art Library:** Nationalmuseum, Stockholm, Sweden (cr). **Corbis:** Alinari Archives (cl); Francis G. Mayer (bc); Hulton-Deutsch Collection (c). **iStockphoto.com:** (t). **59 The Bridgeman Art Library:** Art Gallery of South Australia, Adelaide, Australia (bc); Florence Griswold Museum, Old Lyme, Connecticut, USA/ Gift of the Hartford Steam Boiler Inspection & Insurance Co. (br); Agnew's, London, UK/© Tate, London 2009 (bl); Musee Marmottan, Paris, France / Giraudon (tl). **Corbis:** The Gallery Collection (tc) (c) (cl) (cr) (tr). **60 Alamy Images:** The London Art Archive (br). **The Bridgeman Art Library:** Musee d'Orsay, Paris, France/ Lauros/Giraudon (bc). **Corbis:** Edimédia (bl); The Gallery Collection (clb). **DK Images:** ©Musee Marmottan photo: Susanna Price (ca) (tr). **TopFoto.co.uk:** Roger-Viollet (c). **61 The Bridgeman Art Library:** Musee Marmottan, Paris, France/Giraudon (t). **Corbis:** The Gallery Collection (b); Louvre, Paris, France (bc); Louvre, Paris, France/Giraudon (br). **62 The Bridgeman Art Library:** Louvre, Paris, France/ Lauros/Giraudon (bl); The Detroit Institute of Arts, USA/Gift of Dr. Ernest Stillman (clb). s.moore (tl) (b). **63 The Bridgeman Art Library:** Private Collection/Peter Willi (fbl). **Corbis:** Christie's Images (t) (bl). **East News Poland:** Laski Diffusion (br). **Daniel E. Greene, N.A.:** (fbr). **64 The Bridgeman Art Library:** Private Collection/Christie's Images (c); Van Gogh Museum, Amsterdam, The Netherlands/ Giraudon (clb) (bl). **Corbis:** Joe Epstein/Star Ledger (br); The Gallery Collection (tr). **Getty Images:** Bridgeman Art Library (fcl) (cl) (cr). **http://www.myartnsoulstudio.com/:** (fbr). **65 akg-images. Getty Images:** Hulton Archive (fcr). **66 The Bridgeman Art Library:** Museum of Modern Art, New York, USA (b). **© Tate, London 2009:** Copyright the artist (t). **67 The Bridgeman Art Library:** Musee d'Orsay, Paris, France / Lauros / Giraudon (cl). **Corbis:** Francis G. Mayer (tl). **Getty Images:** Ignacio Auzike (bl); Bridgeman Art Library (br). **© Tate, London 2009:** (tr). **68 Corbis:** The Gallery Collection (bl) (bc) (br); Historical Picture Archive/By kind permission of the Mucha Foundation/The Bridgeman Art Library (t). **69 The Bridgeman Art Library:** Galerie Daniel Malingue, Paris/© DACS 2009 (br). **Corbis:** Burstein Collection (bl); Francis G. Mayer (tr); The Gallery Collection/© ADAGP, Paris and DACS, London 2009 (tl). **Getty Images:** Bridgeman Art Library (tc). **Photo Scala, Florence:** (bc). **70 Alamy Images:** The London Art Archive (cl). **The Bridgeman Art Library:** Rustem Pasa Camii (mosque) Tekirdag, Istanbul, Turkey / © World Religions Photo Library (bl). **Corbis:** Bettmann (c). **70-71** © Succession H. Matisse/DACS 2009. Photo: **© The Bridgeman Art Library**/Musée National d'Art Moderne, Centre Pompidou, Paris, France (t). **71** © Succession H. Matisse/DACS 2009. Photo: **© Tate, London 2009** (br). **72 The Bridgeman Art Library:** Portrait of Dora Maar, Musee Picasso, Paris, France/© Succession Picasso/DACS 2009 (cr); Private Collection/ Roger-Viollet, Paris (t). **Corbis:** Brooklyn Museum (bl); Francis G. Mayer/© Succession Picasso/DACS 2009 (br); The Gallery Collection (cl); The Gallery Collection/© Succession Picasso/DACS 2009 (bc). **Lebrecht Music and Arts:** RA (c). **73 Corbis:** Francis G. Mayer/© Succession Picasso/DACS 2009. **74 The Bridgeman Art Library:** Kettle's Yard, University of Cambridge, UK (cr); Musee National d'Art Moderne, Centre Pompidou, Paris, France/© ADAGP, Paris

This is the palette of Claude Monet, who was fascinated by color. He gave this advice to another painter: "When you go out to paint, try to forget what objects you have before you—a tree, a house, a field, or whatever. Merely think: here is a little square of blue, here is an oblong of pink, here is a streak of yellow, and paint it just as it looks to you, the exact color and shape."